THE STREETCARS AND INTERURBANS OF OLD SANDUSKY, OHIO

by Glenn D. Everett

With best wishes from the author,

Glenn D. Everett

Academy Books

Rutland, Vermont 05701

Library of Congress Card Catalog Number 88-72364

Dedication

This book is affectionately dedicated to the memory of a great local Sandusky historian, Wilbert (Tepe) Ohlemacher (1892-1987). For many years, he wrote a popular column about old times for the Sandusky Sunday Register. When "Tepe" was 93 and failing health made it difficult for him to meet deadlines, the author offered to do a couple of guest columns for him on the subject of how much fun it had been to ride the old city streetcar lines. Unfortunately, before they could be finished, Mr. Ohlemacher passed away a few days after his 94th birthday.

Looking over the material, the author realized there was enough to do a whole book about the old trolley cars. So this is what happened. We are grateful to "Tepe" Ohlemacher for his inspiration and for a lifetime of friendship dating back 60 years to when he was our beloved Sunday School teacher.

Acknowledgements

Helen Hansen, curator of the Follett House Museum, 404 Wayne Street, Sandusky, Ohio, for her valuable help in locating historical data about the early horsecars and streetcar lines.

Anne Gilcher of Sandusky for making available the handwritten notes left by her grandfather, Frank P. Gilcher (1877-1954) whose career spanned more than half a century from streetcar operator in 1896 to many years as general superintendent of the Lake Shore Electric Railway Co. and its successor, the Lake Shore Coach Co. from which he retired in 1951. His recollection of the Herdic omnibus lines operated by his father and uncle are priceless to historians.

Leslie J. Fishel, director emeritus of the Rutherford B. Hayes Presidential Center, Fremont, Ohio, and Gilbert Gonzalez, director of its photograph division, for their assistance in locating old photographs of interurbans.

And, of course, posthumously to Charles E. Frohman (1903-1976), of Sandusky, former president of the Ohio Historical Society, for his indefatigable work in preserving so much of the area's history.

CONTENTS

Thomas A. Edison is shown in his laboratory at Menlo Park, N.J., in this undated photograph taken in the 1880's about the time he was developing an electric dynamo of sufficient power to operate a line of streetcars. Usually depicted only in the formal portrait taken of him at age 82 when the 50th anniversary of his invention of the incandescent electric light bulb was observed nationwide in 1929, this is how a much younger Tom Edison looked when he was making his great inventions. He rarely took time then to pose for pictures.

Chapter One

Sandusky's Streetcars, a Product of Thomas A. Edison

As the 20th Century dawned in 1900, the city of Sandusky could boast one of the most efficient streetcar systems of any city its size. It was also the hub of an electric interurban system that connected it with the cities of Cleveland and Toledo, with a growing number of connections at those points with scores of other cities.

The fact that the city had taken such a position of leadership in providing public transportation was due in no small part to the enthusiastic pride its citizens took in Erie County's most famous native citizen, Thomas Alva Edison.

The streetcar was not directly an invention of Edison, but was a byproduct of a dazzling series of inventions that had made the young inventor a national celebrity.

Tom Edison had come to world renown in 1879 at the age of only 32 when he patented the first electric incandescent bulb. This literally revolutionized life as it had been known for all the centuries of man's existence, for it made it possible to obtain light by simply pushing a switch instead of having to make one's way by flaming torches or candles or by burning oil in a lamp.

The age of electricity had been born and Thomas Edison soon showed an astonished world what it could do to provide light, power, and a number of remarkable things that had never before been possible.

Thomas Alva Edison was born in Milan, a town only 13 miles south of Sandusky, on February 11, 1847, a day now observed nationally by thousands of students at "open house" events in scores of scientific laboratories. He was the seventh

1

and youngest child of Samuel and Nancy Edison and the small brick cottage in which he was born is now a National Historic Site visited by thousands of tourists annually from as far away as India and Japan.

Edison's father was a carpenter who operated a small mill that made wooden shingles for roofs. His mother had been a schoolteacher before her marriage. An extraordinary fact about Edison's career is the brevity of his formal education in school. He was extremely energetic and hated sitting still in school, reciting lessons in unison with the other students. Three months after he entered first grade he brought home a note from his teacher. She said he should not return to school after Christmas as he was "too dense" to learn.

Edison's mother was stung by the note and resolved to teach her son at home, instinctively recognizing that he had an unusually keen and inquisitive mind. She soon taught him to read, and before a year had passed, he was eagerly devouring books far beyond those other children would be finding in school.

The family moved to Port Huron, Michigan, when Edison was seven. His father continued in the shingle business and young Edison kept on reading every book he could get his hands on.

By the time he was 12, young Tom took his first job as a baggage handler on the Grand Trunk Railway which had just completed building a line that linked Port Huron with Detroit. He took over the baggage car and virtually made it his home. His mother had given him a book that explained how new knowledge could be gained by performing scientific experiments. A corner of that baggage car became Edison's first laboratory.

Tom also sold newspapers to passengers who crowded the train. The Civil War broke out in 1861 when Southern states seceded from the Union and formed the Confederate States of America. There was feverish interest in the latest dispatches from the rapidly expanding war front.

At 14, Edison bought a small press and began printing his own newspaper, the Port Huron Herald, in a corner of the baggage car. News from the war front was coming by telegraph. Samuel F.B. Morse had invented the telegraph less than 20 years before and lines were now strung from poles all over the country. But with thousands of young men away in the army, telegraph traffic became so heavy that Edison was frustrated by the fact that messages often came through hours late.

Only one message at a time could be sent along a telegraph wire. Edison learned Morse code and soon became an expert telegrapher. Most of his colleagues accepted the fact that if you had one wire, you could send one message. That seemed a natural law -- but not to Edison. He had just read one of the classic books of early science, "Experimental Research in Electricity," by the pioneer scientist, Michael Faraday. Tom was impressed -- and was off and running.

At 18, Edison was granted his first patent for a device that made faster telegraphy possible. By the time he was 22 he had discovered a way to send two messages at a time on the same wire -- and then four. He abandoned his baggage car and moved to New York City. There at 23 he sold his first big invention, a device that recorded figures on a piece of paper tape. With a telegrapher stationed on the floor of the New York Stock Exchange, this made it possible for brokers and bankers in their offices blocks away to keep up with the latest stock trades, minute-by-minute. It was the first stock ticker, and he sold the patent rights to a group of stockbrokers for $40,000, a handsome sum in those days.

With this money, Edison established a laboratory in West Orange, New Jersey, in an area known as Menlo Park. He hired several young men to assist him and there emerged from his experiments a rapid flurry of inventions that soon caused him to be called by the press "The Wizard of Menlo Park."

After Edison invented the electric light bulb, it was necessary to market it. In 1882 he built a dynamo to generate electricity in a vacant warehouse building in midtown Manhattan and connected 32 customers to it by wires. They used the power it generated to light 400 of the new bulbs.

As Edison steadily increased the size and power of his dynamos he also answered a great need for improved transportation in America's rapidly growing cities.

In 1883, in Kansas City, Missouri, the first successful experiment was conducted in propelling an electric streetcar. By hooking up a dynamo to a wire strung above the street, a car could be propelled. It had a prong with a wheel on top that ran along the wire and the necessary electric circuit was completed by grounding the current of electricity through steel wheels that ran on steel rails. The electric motor was powered by the circuit thus created.

The prong that touched the overhead wire was called a trolley. The era of the trolley car had been born.

Edison went on with a whirlwind of other inventions, including the phonograph, which made it possible to record for the first time a human voice. It was Edison's reciting "Mary Had a Little Lamb." But soon it was the voice of presidents and operatic singers like Enrico Caruso. In 1890 came one of the most remarkable of all his ingenious inventions, the motion picture camera and a projector that could show pictures that moved. The great movie industry came into being.

Small wonder that people back in his native Ohio took great pride in Thomas Edison and were eager to put into use his great inventions.

If Edison said you could draw invisible power from a wire hung over the street and use it to operate horse cars without the horses, they were ready to believe him, astonishing and almost magical as this seemed to people at that time. Investors were ready to dig into their pockets to come up with the large sums necessary to lay tracks, build power plants, and construct cars run with electric motors.

Sandusky welcomed electric streetcars with enthusiasm and soon also interurban cars linking it with many other cities. Erie County was mighty proud of its native son and was ready to buy anything he invented or had helped to develop.

Chapter Two

Clip-Clop Came the Horsecars—But Not for Long

Thomas Edison was not one moment too soon with his development of the electric dynamo as a means of powering electric streetcars.

American cities grew rapidly after the Civil War as the industrialization of America proceeded at a fast pace and thousands of young people left farms to seek jobs in the city. Every ship that sailed into New York harbor brought scores of immigrants seeking new lives of opportunity in the land of freedom.

Sandusky more than quadrupled in population from 1850 to 1890, growing from 5,000 inhabitants to more than 23,000. As the city grew larger, getting to work became a problem. The average person had only one means of transportation, walking on foot. The typical factory worker did not have the means to purchase and feed a horse, nor any place to stable it.

Originally, all of Sandusky's business places and industries were located along the waterfront in the central part of the city. Now, with the waterfront becoming very crowded, new industrial areas were developing alongside the railroad tracks in both the East End and West End.

This created a difficult situation, for a man or woman who lived on the west side of town found it hard to take employment on the east side. It was too far to walk to work and back, particularly on cold winter days. It was getting hard enough as the city expanded to walk downtown to the major stores and offices, and soon a worker was limited in his employment opportunities to the side of the city on which he or she lived.

In addition to this difficulty, another serious problem arose when a new railroad was built through the southern edge of the city in 1872. Until that time, the passenger stations for all five railroads that served the city had been located near the waterfront and were fairly easy to reach. Their tracks all ran where Shoreline Drive is now.

Then the Lake Shore and Michigan Southern Railroad which connected Sandusky with Cleveland built a new track across the south side of the city and erected a new station on a street that was built between Hayes Avenue and Camp Street and named, appropriately enough, North Depot Street.

From the time in 1835 that the Mad River and Lake Erie Railroad broke ground for Ohio's very first railroad in a ceremony attended by Governor William Henry Harrison near East Battery Park, all the railroad stations had been easy to reach. The new one was not.

The Lake Shore and Michigan Southern was one of the earliest railroads, after the Mad River, to serve Sandusky, and built a track from Cleveland that entered the city along the East End waterfront, running on a roadbed erected on fill a little offshore so it could be very straight. This created an area known as the Cove which still exists today, although the raiload track is long gone, and is the site of many boat houses for pleasure craft.

The railroad company also built a line to Toledo, embodying a great engineering project in 1855, the construction of a bridge across Sandusky Bay. The track was built on fill through the marshes west of the village of Venice and then across the bay to Danbury and on to Port Clinton, Oak Harbor and Toledo. It was a very expensive project and when the depression known as the Panic of 1857 struck, the line went into bankruptcy. When it emerged from financial ruin, the costly bridge project was abandoned. Trains still came from Cleveland, but went no farther than Sandusky.

In 1872, Commodore Cornelius Vanderbilt, the great financier in New York City, merged the Lake Shore and Michigan Southern into his New York Central system as he worked toward the goal of a straight, fast connection between New York and Chicago. He rebuilt the bay bridge and rather than have the trains run all the way down to the Sandusky waterfront, constructed a new line that went straight as an arrow from Huron through the south edge of Sandusky.

6

The new station was a long way from downtown. Incoming passengers had to hire a hansom cab to reach the city's major hotels, or to get to their homes. A hansom cab was a horse-drawn carriage which carried passengers for a fee, just as taxicabs do today. Passengers had to send their baggage into the city by dray. A dray was a flatbed wagon which would carry suitcases, trunks and other packages and boxes, as delivery trucks do now. It was pulled by a sturdy team of draft horses.

However, there never seemed to be enough hansom cabs or drays, and passengers often had to wait an hour for one. It was also very inconvenient to get out to the station, and we have to remember that anyone who wanted to go anywhere out of town in the 19th Century had to take a train. There was no other mode of travel available.

The problem became all the worse when it turned out that more people wanted to take Commodore Vanderbilt's fast new rail line than the other railroads that went south and southwest out of Sandusky. The New York Central system gave fast connections to Toledo, Detroit and Chicago in one direction and Cleveland, Buffalo, New York and Boston in the other. More people wanted to go to those destinations than to Columbus, Springfield or Cincinnati, for example.

It is easy to see that the city of Sandusky needed a system of public transportation.

Two enterprising young brothers, Charles A. Gilcher and William H. Gilcher, in 1882 decided to meet this need by establishing an omnibus line. The word "omnibus" comes from Latin and means a wheeled vehicle that carries everyone. An omnibus was a large horse-drawn wagon fitted with a cab covered by a roof with glass windows along the sides.

The Gilchers' omnibuses had small wheels in the front for easy turning, with the driver sitting on a seat above them. The rear wheels were six feet in diameter. The bus was entered by a rear door reached by climbing three steps. Inside around the sides were benches that would seat ten passengers. Three or more could stand, hanging onto a bar suspended from the roof.

People who wanted to ride would stand at a street corner and signal the driver who would rein the horses to a stop and collect the 10-cent fare. The passenger would climb aboard and, with the driver's loud command of "Giddyap!,"

Omnibus 1880s
USA 1c

USA20c

First American streetcar, New York City, 1832

Horse-drawn omnibus as illustrated on the one-cent coil stamp issued in 1986 by the U.S. Postal Service and (below) an early New York City horsecar depicted on a 20-cent stamp in 1983.

the horses would take off. There was a small bell inside which a passenger could ring to signal the driver that he wished to get off at the next corner.

The omnibus was not very comfortable to ride as it bumped and jolted over the unpaved streets. Water Street, which was paved with rough cobblestones was the only paved street in Sandusky in the early days. The others were smoothed a little each spring with horse-drawn graders and oil was sprinkled on to keep down the summer dust.

In the winter, however, when the streets were covered with snow, the Gilchers substituted runners for wheels and the omnibuses were turned into big sleighs. That must have been fun to ride. The buses were not heated, but straw was placed on the floor to keep cold air from coming in the cracks.

Frank Gilcher, Charles' seven-year-old son, later recalled how he and his friends enjoyed sifting through the straw to find coins that passengers had dropped. In fact, Frank became so infatuated with the idea of public transportation that he became a conductor in 1896 on one of Sandusky's first electric streetcars and later had a 46-year career with the Lake Shore Electric lines as superintendent of its Sandusky-Norwalk division. He continued in that capacity with the Lake Shore Coach Lines which eventually succeeded the streetcar lines, operating motorbus routes.

The Gilcher Brothers called their service the Herdic Lines. They operated three lines on a 20-minute schedule. The first started at the West House at Columbus Avenue and Water Street. The West House was Sandusky's largest hotel, and was torn down in 1926 to become the site of the State Theater. This line went out to serve the new railroad depot, operating south on Columbus Avenue to Washington Row; then, turning west, it stopped in front of the Sloane House, the city's other major hotel. The omnibus then turned left and went out Central Avenue to North Depot Street and came back from the depot by the same route.

The second line served the East End, turning left on Washington Row, and thence out Huron Avenue one block to Hancock Street and out Hancock to Milan Road and then out past Perkins Avenue to the main gate of Oakland Cemetery, where it turned around and went back to the city.

The third route served the West End. It started at the corner of East Washington Street and Meigs Street, in front

9

of the old Waterworks pumping plant. This later become the site of Sandusky's city hall and police headquarters. The line went the length of Washington Street and then out Tiffin Avenue to Mills Street where it turned around for the return journey.

Sanduskians flocked to use the Herdic Lines because it saved them much walking.

The Gilcher Brothers were so successful that they immediately attracted competition. In 1883, a group of Sandusky businessmen formed the Sandusky Street Railway Company and obtained permission from the city government to start laying track for a horsecar line. Horsecars operated on steel rails. They glided along with much less friction and offered a smoother, faster ride. A horsecar could carry as many as 18 passengers.

The first horsecar started up Columbus Avenue from the West House on August 3, 1883, carrying a group of city officials and business leaders, who pronounced the new mode of transportation a wonderful improvement that made Sandusky a truly modern urban center.

The tracks went up Columbus Avenue to Hayes Avenue, out Hayes to North Depot Street and the new depot. There the car reversed direction and returned downtown.

Soon the railway company extended its tracks to form a loop by going all the way across North Depot Street to Camp Street, then down Camp to Washington Street, east on Washington to Jackson, around the corner to West Washington Row and a connection with the Columbus Avenue track.

In 1888, the Gilcher Brothers gave up the competition and the omnibuses rode off into history after only six years of service.

Clip-clop went the horsecars. The line prospered and soon there were seven cars and 28 horses -- 14 husky teams -- housed in a large barn built on Hayes Avenue near the intersection with North Depot. A spur line was added out Columbus Avenue to Scott Street to serve the Erie County fairgrounds during fair time and on days of sulky races. The fairgrounds were located then between Columbus Avenue and Milan Road south of Scott Street. Around 1900, when the fairgrounds were moved to a larger location on Camp Street near Perkins Avenue, a subdivision named Cable Park was built. Cable Park has recently been named a National His-

A horsecar in 1883 prepares to start its run up Columbus Avenue from the West House (at right) then Sandusky's largest hotel. The track of the Mad River and Lake Erie Railroad is in the foreground. The little horsecars could carry a maximum of 14 people out to the new railroad station on North Depot Street.

toric area because of the impressive architecture of its beautiful turn-of-the-century homes.

Days of glory for the horsecars were to be short, however, for even as the line got underway in 1883, experiments were being conducted on running streetcars with electric motors rather than horsepower. Experiments were also undertaken to run them with steam engines, but boilers were bulky and the engines belched smoke and cinders which could start fires, and ashes fell on the streets. Steam engines also made too much noise. Electricity, smooth, clean and quiet, was to be the mode of power for the future.

As soon as Edison's dynamo had improved to the point where it could provide strong, steady electric power, the day of the horsecar was coming to an end.

In 1889, a group of Sandusky businessmen, with great faith in Edison's latest experiments, organized the People's Electric Railway Company and began laying track for an electric streetcar line. They erected a building on the east side of Lawrence Street between Market and Water Streets to house their electric generating plant and to serve as a car barn. Later, this building was occupied for many years by the Sandusky Nut Company, a manufacturer of nuts and bolts whose name always drew a chuckle from passersby. The structure was razed in the 1970s by the Sandusky Foundry and machine Company when it took over that entire block.

The People's Electric laid track on West Market Street to Pearl Street and up Pearl to Tiffin Avenue, then out Tiffin Avenue to Mills Street. In the other direction, they laid a track on Lawrence street to West Water, then east on Water Street all the way to Wayne Street. The track went up Wayne Street one block, then out East Market to Franklin Street and south on Franklin.

The reason for choosing Franklin Street was to serve the depot of the Baltimore and Ohio Railroad which had been built on Warren Street at East Washington. The railroad tracks came down the center of Warren Street so there was no room to put the trolley line there and the line was built one block west on Franklin Street.

The first electric cars began operating in 1890. These included a rather ungainly double-decked car in summer which proved popular because you could sit up under an awning on the roof and enjoy the breeze. In the days before air conditioning, this was a way to escape the stifling heat of a hot evening.

People's Electric soon extended its track up Franklin Street as far as the broad intersection with Huron Avenue and then turned west one block on East Madison Street to Hancock Street. The track then turned south to Milan Road all the way past Perkins Avenue to the gate of Oakland Cemetery.

Meanwhile, the Sandusky Street Railway Company moved quickly to substitute electric cars for the horsecars on its line and in 1893 the clip-clop of the horses pulling the horsecars was no longer to be heard. Less than ten years after it started operation, electric motors had replaced the horses. The street cleaning crews who were busy men in those days of horse-drawn vehicles were grateful because the streetcars left no trail of horse manure behind.

Another major development intensified the need for public transportation in Sandusky. The Ohio state legislature selected a 300-acre site between Columbus Avenue and Milan Road a mile-and-a-half south of Sandusky as the location for a home to care for elderly Civil War veterans. The Ohio Soldiers and Sailors Home, now called the Ohio Veterans Home, opened its doors in 1889. A company was soon organized to provide a connection to downtown Sandusky by electric streetcars. An electric generating plant and car barn was constructed on the east side of Columbus Avenue just south of Perkins Avenue, a site now occupied by the Erie County Highway Department garages and maintenance shop. Track was laid from the north gate of the Soldiers Home on newly constructed DeWitt Avenue, then the main gate for the Home to Columbus Avenue, and along the boulevard on the east side of Columbus Avenue all the way to Scott Street.

There the passengers would have to transfer from the electric car to the horsecar line that would take them the rest of the distance to the downtown business district or to the various train depots.

The horsecars were soon replaced by electric cars, but the transfer point remained the same for several years. The Soldiers Home line soon extended its tracks to Milan Road and then down the east side of Milan Road to the gate of Oakland Cemetery. A picture taken in 1893 of one of its open-air summertime cars appears on the cover of this book.

In 1893, a new company called the Sandusky, Milan, Avery and Norwalk Railroad took over this line and began an audacious project, Ohio's first interurban line. When it was completed in the summer of 1893, it stretched for 16 miles from the Soldiers Home to the city of Norwalk. At that time, it was the nation's longest interurban line.

An interesting feature of this line was the fact that it went down into the deep Huron River Valley and climbed the steep Milan Hill within sight of the little home in which Thomas Edison had been born just 46 years before. The village of Milan was bursting with civic pride as the first car, somewhat to the astonishment of skeptical observers, succeeded in climbing the Milan Hill with the greatest of ease. The magical power of electricity brought gasps of amazement from those who thought that the horse could never be replaced.

One of the mysteries of history is why the electric line was known as the Sandusky, Milan, Avery and Norwalk when, in fact, the village of Avery came first before the line reached Milan. This was not very logical to have the towns listed out of order. Was it because Milan had become so famous as Edison's birthplace that they wanted to put its name first? Or did the sign painter make a mistake when the cars were given their final coat of paint and the proprietors just decided to go along with it?

The village of Avery was an important little town in 1893 with a station on the main line of the Nickel Plate Railroad. The railroad is still there and is now the major east-west line of the Norfolk Southern Railway system between Buffalo and Chicago. The Nickel Plate got its name from the shiny metal fittings of its elegant passenger cars and sleeping cars which operated between Chicago and New York City. The railroad liked the nickname it soon acquired and actually adopted it as its official name for nearly 100 years before vanishing into the era of railroad mergers.

Avery itself suffered a sad fate. When engineers began designing the Ohio Turnpike in 1950, the first great fast four-lane toll road to cross northern Ohio, they announced sadly that there was no way they could cross the deep Huron River Valley without coming straight through the little village. Seventeen homes, nearly all of them examples of beautiful Victorian architecture, had to be demolished or moved. All that remains of Avery now is a few scattered houses and a cluster of motels and filling stations at the interchange of U.S. 250 (the old Milan Road) and the Turnpike, with the big grain elevator still alongside the railroad tracks.

The extremely tall interurban poles made necessary by early-day double-decker cars still stand like sentries on the west side of Milan Road where it passes the Ohio Veterans Home. A sidewalk has been laid where the track once ran.

Photograph 1988 by Glenn D. Everett

15

Double deck streetcars such as Car No. 14 of the Soldiers Home and
Oakland Cemetery line proved popular in summer in the 1890's but required
very high trolley wires and tall poles to carry the lines. The double-deckers
eventually proved to be impractical but the very high poles they required
remain in place nearly a century later.

Hayes Presidential Center
Charles E. Frohman Collection

The village of Milan has retained its architectural integ-
rity and its quiet town square and is regarded as one of the
most beautiful and historical towns in Ohio.

When the interurban line to Norwalk was constructed, poles
of extraordinary height were installed because the line for
a number of years ran double-decker interurban cars. The
trolley above the double-decker had to be suspended quite
high -- and the power lines were even higher above the
trolley wire. These stately poles remain highly visible
along U.S. Route 250, nearly a century after being put in
place. They carry electric power wires to serve homes and
businesses in the area and they dwarf the newer utility
poles put in place near them.

16

The Norwalk interurban enjoyed instant success and heralded the onset of a busy era of track laying all over Ohio and adjoining states as new interurban lines blossomed like dandelion blooms after a rain.

The Lake Shore Electric Company was organized to build a line from Cleveland to Toledo and then on to Detroit. The new electric railway chose Sandusky as its hub. The interurban cars entered Sandusky by way of the Soldiers Home and came down Columbus Avenue to the downtown center. They then left by way of the People's Electric line to Tiffin Avenue and Mills Street from which point the Lake Shore laid tracks out to Venice Road and along Venice Road until it took off cross-country to Castalia, Fremont and eventually Toledo.

With four competing electric car lines in Sandusky, the time had obviously come for consolidation, and the Lake Shore Electric Railway absorbed its competitors, one by one, through merger.

People's Electric, which had been dubbed the "White Line" because of the color of its cars, was in the process of intensifying the competition by building a line straight down Market Street when merger talks intervened. The track reached only as far as the corner of West Market and Fulton Street when work was stopped.

As a result of the consolidation, the old horse car line of the Sandusky Street Railway, now electrified, abandoned its track between Lawrence Street and Columbus Avenue, with the track along West Washington Row and West Washington Street between Jackson and Lawrence Streets being torn up. Meanwhile, the People's Electric also tore up its West Market and Pearl Street lines.

The Tiffin Avenue line now connected directly with West Washington Street and all cars, including the interurbans, turned down Lawrence Street to Water Street.

West Market street had been paved with brick and for years the center of the street had bricks of a different color where the old streetcar track had been removed. The outline can still be seen in the form of a ripple in the asphalt pavement later applied to cover the rather rough bricks.

The Lake Shore Electric Railway consolidated all the car barns and repair facilities at the Norwalk line's car barns on the east side of Columbus Avenue just south of Perkins Avenue. This became the hub of a large system of electric transportation. By 1902, the Sandusky city streetcar system had been completed with construction of a line out East Monroe Street and First Street as far as Lane Street to serve the East End industrial area and a line out West Monroe Street to Superior Street, then the city line, which served the new West End factories. It was thus possible to reach every section of the city without having to walk a long distance.

Now if you will climb into our "time machine," we will take our readers back more than half a century and you can all have a great time joining the author for a ride on each of the city's streetcar lines, as well as excursions to Norwalk, Cleveland and Toledo on the big interurban cars.

The great Trolley Car Era has passed into history. Even as it started in the early 1890s, Henry Ford and others were tinkering with "horseless carriages," powered by sputtering, backfiring gasoline motors that were eventually to do to the electric streetcars what they had just done to the horse-cars. But while it lasted, the Trolley Car Era was an exciting time and it was a lot of fun to ride the cars.

The NYC depot, once the busiest spot in town, now stands vacant waiting for a new buyer to convert it to a restaurant or other purpose.

Sandusky Register 1988

Chapter Three

An Exciting Ride to the Soldiers' Home

If horsecars lasted only a decade in Sandusky, the electric streetcars were destined to be much more successful. Sanduskians began riding them early and for nearly 50 years the little orange cars with their clanging bells were an important part of the city's life.

The streetcars bridged the gap between the time the average citizen had to walk anywhere he wished to go in the city to the day when a rising standard of living made it possible for most families to own an automobile.

Where did the streetcar lines go in Sandusky and what was it like to ride them? Well, step into our "time machine" and we will push a button that will send us back about 60 years. We will find the streetcars again rolling down the street and go for a ride.

For our first trip, let's go out to the Soldiers Home because that is the longest ride and one of the most interesting.

To catch our car, we will have to go downtown to the interurban station. The first station for the Lake Shore Electric's interurban cars, as well as for the city's streetcar lines, was in a building at the corner of Columbus Avenue and Market Street. The structure was later the site of a busy S.S. Kresge five-and-ten cent store -- in a day when most items in the store could be purchased for a nickel or a dime. Later it became a Jupiter Discount Store before falling vacant, as did most of the other downtown stores, after suburban shopping malls were built.

About 1920, the interurban station was moved to a new building on the West side of Columbus Avenue between Market and Water Streets. Since 1947, it has been the location of

This building at the southeast corner of Columbus Avenue and East Market Street housed Sandusky's first interurban station. Later it became an S.S. Kresge 5 and 10 cents store and its successor, a Jupiter discount store. When photographed in 1988, it had fallen vacant, as had many other downtown retail establishments.

Photograph 1988 by Glenn D. Everett

Marv Byers' clothing store. So it is to this location, just south of Sandusky's beautiful and then brand-new State Theater, that we shall go in our "time machine" to take a streetcar ride.

We will find the interurban station to be one of the busiest places in town. A man behind a big counter in the rear is selling interurban tickets and tokens for the city streetcars. They are embossed steel discs which offer a discount to frequent passengers. The fare is 10 cents cash or three tokens for a quarter, a dozen for a dollar. We make our way past more than a dozen people sitting on wooden benches, waiting for the next interurban car, and purchase some tokens.

Almost every city streetcar line in the country at this time used tokens to reward frequent riders. The tokens were usually embossed with the name of the transit line and had a letter or logo symbol to identify them so that riders could not use tokens purchased in one city to take a ride on a car line in another. Collectors in those days liked to get as many tokens as they could from different lines to show how many cities they had visited. A few such collections have survived and today are quite valuable. If someone were to find some old Sandusky streetcar tokens, they would be worth much more than three for a quarter. Their use in Sandusky was discontinued and paper tickets substituted when fares were raised, and none are known to exist, but some collector may someday come up with one.

With our token in hand, we step outside on the sidewalk by the busy newsstand and in a few minutes a car comes around the corner from East Water Street and the sign on its front reads "Soldiers Home via Milan Road."

The Soldiers Home was connected with downtown Sandusky by a loop line. You could go either by way of Columbus Avenue or Milan Road. Since we are just going for a sightseeing

An early Sandusky city streetcar photographed at the Soldiers Home. The car is of wooden construction. Steel cars of about the same size replaced these about 1920.

Hayes Presidential Center
Charles E. Frohman Collection

ride, it does not make any difference which car comes first and we will take the one that goes by Milan Road.

Sandusky's streetcars stopped at any corner where a passenger hailed them or where someone on the car wanted to disembark. Therefore, the Soldiers Home line provided transportation for a considerable segment of the city and not just out to the Soldiers Home and back.

By the 1920s, the original wooden streetcars had been replaced by more modern cars built of steel. These were rounded in front -- one might almost say streamlined -- and with their improved springs and shock absorbers were much more comfortable than the early cars which tended to jolt and jerk along very noisily, especially over switches. In fact, the new steel cars were much more comfortable than the small city buses which eventually replaced them. They also were cleaner and did not emit obnoxious diesel exhaust fumes to pollute the air. Electric streetcars were quiet, clean and very energy efficient.

As our car comes to a stop on the track in the center of the street, our motorman opens the front door which operates by compressed air and makes a loud hiss-s-s as it folds open. We wait for passengers on board to step down before we climb up the three steps to the car and drop our tokens -- tinkle, tinkle -- in the glass-enclosed fare box, as the motorman watches to make sure everyone is dropping in the correct fare.

Some passengers hand him a little colored slip of paper called a "transfer." Passengers who wish to transfer to another line can get one from the motorman, provided they are going to continue in the same direction. The transfers are printed on a different color paper each day and are torn off in a length that indicates the hour at which they were issued. The later in the day, the longer the transfer slip. This is to make certain that the passengers use their transfers for just one ride across the city and do not try to save them to take a free ride on another line or another day.

Streetcar systems in various cities used transfers of different styles and designs, so a hobby grew up collecting them as well as tokens. These hobbyists call themselves "pedamographers," a fancy name for an old hobby, just as stamp collectors call themselves "philatelists" and coin collectors "numismatists." If anyone were to find an old Sandusky streetcar transfer, this would be a prize to such a collector.

We have dropped our tokens in the fare box and will take seats on the left side, as the view from that window will be more exciting at one point in our ride.

Other passengers come aboard and our motorman closes the door with another loud "hiss-s-s" of compressed air. Then there is a further hiss of air as he releases the brakes. Compressed air was a very important element in the operation of an electric streetcar. We now notice that the motorman uses only his hands in operating the car. He turns a handle on the panel in front of him and the farther he advances it, the faster we move. He reaches for a valve handle to apply air to the brakes when we stop. In the event of an emergency he can also reverse the motor and the wheels will spin backward on the track amidst a shower of sparks. This will stop us in a hurry. He opens the door with another little handle and uses his foot only to ring the bell that warns people to get off the track ahead.

Motormen did not have to steer a streetcar, as the track took care of determining the direction it was going to move.

Our streetcar starts up Columbus Avenue, but only for a short distance. At the corner of Market Street we are going to turn east and here we can see our motorman operate an interesting device that will flip the switch automatically. Originally, electric streetcars were designed exactly like horsecars, except that the motorman, who stood on a platform out on the front of the car, had no reins to the horses to hold any longer, but a handle that operated the motor. When he reached a switch, he had a long steel pole that he poked down in a hole and threw the switch by hand. When the new steel cars came along in the 1920s, they had a switch that activated a magnetic device that threw the switch automatically with a loud "click."

In fact, operating a streetcar in the 1920s had become much easier. The motorman now sat inside the car which was heated in the winter by electric coils in boxes along the edges of the floor, rather than with a wood-fired potbelly stove as was the case with the earlier cars. He had a broad windshield to protect him from wind and rain.

An interesting footnote of Ohio history is the fact that in 1906, motormen in Columbus went on strike, demanding that they be given enclosed platforms on which to work in the bitter cold days of winter. One of the leaders of the strike was Frank Nixon, who became father of a President of the United States. When Richard M. Nixon was running for President he used to recall this story, especially when seeking votes from labor union members. The elder Mr. Nixon later left Ohio for Whittier, California, where he operated a small family grocery and where the future President Nixon was born in 1913.

Our car, with its comfortable motorman, now moves along East Market Street and stops at the corner of Wayne Street to pick up some more passengers, several of whom carry shopping bags full of groceries and other items they have purchased in the busy downtown stores. Our motorman again throws a switch so that we go straight out East Market instead of turning down Wayne Street.

As we approach Hancock Street, he throws another switch. We are approaching a single section of track that will carry us for the next eight blocks. On one of the poles that supports our trolley wire, there is a little light that shows green, indicating that the track is clear ahead of us. The motorman pushes a switch that will turn a light red on a pole near the corner of Hancock and East Monroe Streets to warn a car coming in the opposite direction that we are on the single track section. In the old days, the motorman had to climb out of the car and go over to the pole, unlock a box and push the switch by hand. The box was kept locked to prevent vandals from tampering with it and causing two cars to approach one another head-on.

American railroads today might do well to take a look at the old system of signals used by the Sandusky streetcar systems 60 years ago, since there is no record that any cars ever collided head-on at any of the single-track sections of the lines. Railroads today seem to have collisions and derailments almost every other month because they get two trains on one track.

We proceed safely now over the switch that takes us down to a single track and go out on East Market to the corner of Franklin Street. We then go south on Franklin, stopping at Washington Street to pick up some passengers, carrying suitcases, who have just come from the Baltimore and Ohio (B. & O. for short) station at the corner of Warren and Washington Streets one block away.

As we continue up Franklin Street, the motorman calls off the streets. "Adams Street," he says, "Jefferson Street! Huron Avenue!"

Now we come to a place where the motorman is going to proceed very carefully. The big broad intersection ahead brings together Huron Avenue, Franklin Street, Elm Street and East Madison Street. When Sandusky was originally laid out in 1818, the streets formed a pattern based on the traditional logo of the Masonic Lodge. Elm Street, crossing Huron Avenue diagonally at that point, represents the calipers that are part of the Masonic badge. On the west side of the city, the intersection of Central Avenue with Poplar Street, Fulton Street, and West Madison creates a similar broad intersection and represents the other side of the calipers.

Our streetcar has to enter the Huron Avenue intersection very carefully, for we are not just going to cross this busy thoroughfare, but make a sweeping right turn that will take us into East Madison Street. In the days of the horse and carriage when this track was laid down in 1892, this did not create a problem. But before the line was abandoned in the 1930s, it had become very hazardous. Automobiles were now coming from all directions, particularly from both ways on Huron Avenue, which before the days of the Sandusky Bypass of Route 2, not only carried all the traffic of this busy route from Toledo to Cleveland, but also carried U.S. Route 6, a highway that had been laid out all the way from Portland, Maine, to Portland, Oregon. This route carried a great deal of through traffic from Chicago to Buffalo and upstate New York. Thus, Huron Avenue had become an extremely busy street.

The fact that streetcars made a turn as they crossed this intersection often caught automobile drivers by surprise. Loud as the motormen might ring their bells, it was still the scene of a number of fender-benders between streetcars and autos.

We can breathe a sigh of relief as we make it safely through this intersection, despite the squeal of brakes as a couple of autoists suddenly note that we are changing direction as we cross it.

Our car proceeds just one block on East Madison to Hancock Street and then turns left. Here we come to a block of double tracks and, sure enough, a streetcar coming in the opposite direction has been waiting for us to clear the single-track section. As soon as we round the corner and move on to the right hand track, the car to our left goes on to the single track section, heading north. In a moment that motorman will be clanging his bell furiously as he moves through the Huron Avenue intersection. Let's hope he makes it.

Meanwhile, our car pauses at East Monroe Street where some passengers, clutching transfers from the East Monroe line, climb aboard. With a loud rumble, our car crosses over the East Monroe line's tracks as we proceed south.

We move back onto a long single-track section now and our motorman throws a switch that will turn a light red way out at the intersection of Milan Road and Soldiers Home. We move up the center of Hancock Street on our single track and pause to drop off a passenger at the intersection of Scott Street. We now angle slightly to the left and are on Milan Road, the name of our street having changed.

In one more block we come to another hazardous place in our ride. At this point, two tracks of the B. & O. Railroad cross Milan Road at a very oblique angle. The B. & O. tracks, now abandoned and torn up, ran up the center of Warren Street as far as East Madison and then angled slightly to the right. By the time we reach the intersection of Finch Street and Milan Road, we find these tracks crossing at a long slanting angle.

Our motorman has to be very cautious. By law, he is obliged to open the door and actually step down and look both ways on the tracks to make certain no train is coming. There is a switch engine 100 yards to our left, but it is just moving some cars onto the track in the Weier Brothers salvage yard (or "junk yard" as we used to call it) where a big crane with a magnet will fill those cars with iron and steel scrap for the mills. Our motorman, after ascertaining that the switch engine will not be coming toward us to cross Milan Road, hops back into his seat and, with a considerable clatter and jolting, we cross the two tracks of the B. & O.

At this point, our streetcar leaves the center of the street. We are going to operate for several blocks on the boulevard at the right of the street. We make one interesting stop, as we pick up some workers who have just completed their shift at a big lumber yard. Then called the Garretson Lumber Co., it has since been the Apel Lumber Co. and now the Carter Lumber Co. The fragrant odor of freshly cut lumber was always pleasant when the streetcar stopped at the lumber yard's wide front door.

At Sycamore Line, our tracks changed to the left side of Milan Road. Here, in the old days, came one of the really scary parts of the ride. At that time, there was a large abandoned stone quarry which stretched from Milan Road down Sycamore Line to Cleveland Road, which had just been constructed along the north edge of the quarry. The quarry was 30 or 40 feet deep in places and the stone removed from it had been used in the construction of many of the fine old houses and commercial buildings of early Sandusky. Abandoned by the 1920s, it was gradually being filled in by what we called the "town dump," but which is now called a "landfill" as if that was something a little more sanitary. Actually what went into the old quarry in those days was largely ashes and cinders from the hundreds of coal stoves that heated Sandusky homes before the days of centralized heating with gas or oil.

By the 1920s, the Wagner Quarry two miles farther south on Milan Road, just south of the Soldiers Home, had replaced the abandoned quarry as a source of stone for the Sandusky area. As we look out the left windows of our streetcar, we cannot see the tracks underneath our car, nor the rather thin shelf of stone on which they were laid alongside Milan Road. We can see directly down into the deep chasm and it seems we are perilously close to its edge. Obviously, the side of the quarry excavation was strong and did not erode, for no streetcars ever fell into it. But they had laid the track mighty close to the edge, more confident of its safety than were some of the riders.

Now our streetcar arrives at a real hazard, not at all a figment of the imagination. We are going to have to cross the four tracks of the New York Central Railroad. This was the main line between New York and Chicago and both passenger and freight trains moved at a very high speed along it. The two tracks in the center carried the fast limiteds, while the tracks at the sides carried the slower-moving local trains and freight trains.

Here our motorman dismounts and looks very carefully both ways. This was particularly true in the early evening hours when the fastest train in America, the Twentieth Century Limited, came roaring out of the West, bound for New York City on a schedule that carried it over 900 miles from Chicago in 18 hours.

The Twentieth Century was the most elegant and prestigious train in the nation. The most prominent people in the country, including movie stars, millionaire business executives, United States Senators, and others rode its well-appointed first class lounge cars, dining cars and overnight suites in its Pullman sleeping cars. The engineer had to slow to 30 miles per hour to cross the Sandusky Bay bridge, but when he reached the straightaway through Venice, Sandusky and Huron, he opened the throttle wide, and if he was five or ten minutes behind schedule, this is where he made it up.

The top speed of the Twentieth Century is said to have been 70 miles per hour. Those who watched the awesome sight as this train passed through Sandusky can swear that it sometimes appeared to be closer to 100 miles per hour. The train was moving so fast that its whistle was blowing continuously as it approached the Campbell Street, Columbus Avenue, Milan Road and Pipe Street grade crossings. The westbound Twentieth Century from New York to Chicago passed through Sandusky in the early morning hours.

Other passenger trains went through Sandusky at high speeds, but none were as impressive as the Twentieth Century at full throttle. In any event, the motormen on Sandusky streetcars were very cautious when they crossed the tracks of the New York Central.

If the belching black smoke of a train was to be seen coming down the track, the motorman simply returned to his seat and waited for the other train to pass. He was under strict instructions to take no chances. When a train had passed, he again dismounted from the car and looked in both directions to make certain no other train was coming.

Once assured, the motorman very quickly sends our little car scurrying across the tracks with bumping and clicking as we hurry over them.

Safely across the tracks, we proceed south along Milan Road, stopping at Perkins Avenue, and again opposite the main gate of the big Oakland Cemetery where a passenger, carrying a wreath to place on the grave of a loved one, disembarks and crosses the road.

Our car goes on out Milan Road and when it reaches DeWitt Avenue, our track turns and we join the track that runs along the fence on the north side of the Home's grounds. From our left a track joins us that carries the interurbans from Norwalk and Cleveland and, as we reach a stretch of double track in front of what was then the main gate of the home, we see an interurban heading for Cleveland that has just picked up some passengers and waited a moment for us to pull alongside. Behind the interurban is another city streetcar that will be going back down Milan Road the way we have just come.

The Soldiers Home station is a busy place. Several of our passengers get off. Some veterans who live at the home get on to ride downtown. A couple are very elderly gentlemen, who obviously are veterans of the Civil War of more than 60 years before, on their way to do a little socializing at the Grand Army of the Republic hall which was in the Cooke block on the east side of Columbus Avenue just north of Market Street.

Some other gray-haired veterans get on. They are from the Spanish-American War of 1898. Maybe they rode with Theodore Roosevelt's Rough Riders. One of them wearing a broad-brimmed cowboy-style hat may be a Veteran of the Indian Wars. In those days, there were always half a dozen or so veterans who qualified because of service with the cavalry out on the Plains. What stories they could tell us of the Old West! Tall ones, sometimes, but nonetheless exciting, we may be sure.

A few younger men also board our trolley. They are in their 30s or 40s, veterans of World War I, who were beginning to fill the beds at the Home left vacant by the passing of the old Civil War veterans. Many of them are coughing, their lungs ruined by gas warfare in the trenches of France in 1918.

With all of our new passengers aboard, we take off, once again watching a signal to make certain that two miles of single-track line ahead of us are clear. We move along the

Streetcars and interurbans operated on the boulevard on the east side of Columbus Avenue. Today looking south from the intersection of Finch Street and Columbus Avenue, we can clearly see where the track lay. The poles that carried the trolley wire remain in place now carrying telephone and electric power lines.

Photograph 1988 by Glenn D. Everett

south side of DeWitt Avenue, then turn north, operating on the boulevard on the east side of Columbus Avenue.

Now if we can slip into a couple of empty seats on the right side of the car, we will see yet another exciting view, as we pass the car barns.

We first pass the large stone building of the Erie County Infirmary, the old people's home, and we wave to a couple of white-bearded gentlemen who sit on the benches and enjoy exchanging greetings with the streetcar passengers who pass by. Then the car barns come in sight. A line branches off from our track and as it enters the car yards, branches into half a dozen more. Way in the back we see the repair shop where the cars can be raised up on hoists to repair their brakes and wheels. At the side of the shops are the tracks where the spare cars are stored, including some of the old open trolleys no longer used. Even in the 1920s these look very old-fashioned, indeed. We get quite a view of the car barns as we pass by and stop to pick up a couple of workers who have finished their shift and who flash an employee's pass to the motorman who lets them on for a free ride.

Now our car reaches Perkins Avenue and we are back in the city. We continue along the boulevard until we reach the New York Central tracks which we have to cross again. Not only do we cross the four tracks of the New York Central, but this is a very complex crossing because the B. & O. track also crosses diagonally at this point. So our motorman has to be especially careful because trains can come from four directions!

There is a watchman in a signal tower to our left who raises and lowers gates when trains are coming, but this is the one place where there was once a collision between an interurban car and a B. & O. switch engine which sideswiped it and knocked it right over on its side. No one was killed, but it was a warning of the catastrophe that could occur at the point where all these tracks crossed. Undoubtedly, it hastened the building of the Columbus Avenue subway which was undertaken in 1926.

The subway was unique because it was the only such structure in the nation where two railroads actually crossed each other on top of the subway. This unique feature of construction can still be seen although now the B. & O. Railroad has been abandoned

Both streetcars and interurbans used the subway after it was built. A double track was constructed, one track going under each side of the center posts. The double tracks continued as far as Perkins Avenue where they merged back into a single track and moved to the east side of the road on the boulevard.

The old single track was left in place, however, along the boulevard on the east side of Columbus Avenue from Boalt Street north to Scott Street where it moved out into the center of Columbus Avenue and became a double track again.

One reason for this is that Columbus Avenue would have needed to be widened substantially to accommodate a double streetcar track in the middle and this was deemed too expensive to undertake. So when the subway was completed, the streetcars and interurbans went back to a single track alongside Columbus Avenue. The wide lawns on that side of the avenue in front of the distinguished turn-of-the-century homes still show clearly where the interurban track ran more than half a century ago.

Our car now moves out into the center of the street and at Hayes Avenue the tracks of the Depot line join us. A block farther on, the tracks of the East Monroe Street car line meet and merge with us. In five more blocks we are downtown. Our motorman flips the switch at the corner of East Market Street so that we can go east one block, then we turn north onto Wayne Street and go around the corner onto East Water Street and then, at Columbus Avenue, turn left. So here we are back at the interurban station where we started. We hop down the steps, having enjoyed the most adventurous ride the Sandusky streetcar system offered. We got our eight and one-third cents worth, didn't we?

Streetcar tracks were very similar to railroad tracks. When Columbus Avenue was repaved in 1925, the horsecar tracks laid in 1883 were replaced with stronger rails. Workers are seen in this photograph laying the switch that would enable cars to turn onto East Market Street. The track at left temporarily carried interurbans and city streetcars while the work was in progress. The new tracks were then firmly cemented into place and remain under the pavement in the center of Columbus Avenue half a century after the streetcars stopped running.

Hayes Presidential Center
Charles E. Frohman Collection

Chapter Four

Around the Loop on the Depot Line

Are we ready for our next streetcar ride? O.K., let's step into our "time machine," push a button, and we will magically be transported back 60 years. As we look around, we will see that the streetcars are still running on the tracks in the Sandusky streets and we will be able to take a ride all around the loop on the Depot line.

This line served the busiest depot in town, the New York Central depot on North Depot Street. The streetcar connected it with two other railroad depots on West Water Street, the Big Four and the Pennsylvania, as well as with the Baltimore and Ohio depot on Warren Street, via transfer to the Soldiers Home/Milan Road line.

Remember that back in the 1920s, if a person wanted to travel any distance at all, one had to go by train. Although automobiles were rapidly being improved from the wheezing two-cylinder horseless carriages that first appeared around 1900, and major roads were being paved, it was still unthinkable to try to drive all the way to Milwaukee or Kansas City or Philadelphia, for instance, by automobile. Breakdowns were frequent; tire blow-outs common; and garages with mechanics who knew anything about fixing cars still were few and far between, as were filling stations. Passenger travel by airplane was something most people thought belonged strictly in the science fiction category.

Folks still held their breath when the daily mail plane flew over. It wisely flew along the lake shore rather than taking the short cut from Cleveland to Detroit across Lake Erie, since a cow pasture might be handy in which to land in the event of motor trouble. Therefore, if you wanted to travel anywhere, you went by train and the depots were very busy places.

To catch our car on the depot line, we go again from Columbus Avenue to the interurban station in the building which now for a generation has housed Marv Byers' popular clothing store. We buy some more of our bargain three-for-a-quarter tokens and go outside where we can see a little orange car come around the corner from West Water Street, carrying a window sign that simply says "Depot."

We go out into the street, but wait while a dozen passengers get off, many of them carrying suitcases and packages. Some are hugged and kissed by greeting relatives while others trudge off up the street toward the downtown hotels.

We hop on, put our tokens in the fare box, spot some empty seats and, as we sit down, the motorman closes the door and up Columbus Avenue we go.

We stop at Market Street and again at Washington Row while passengers who have been shopping in downtown stores board our car. As with the Soldiers Home line, this car will stop at any corner to take on or let off passengers and thus it serves a large area of the city, as well as connecting with train depots.

Out Columbus Avenue our car goes. At the corner of Monroe Street we stop for a number of passengers clutching transfers from the two Monroe Street lines to climb aboard. A block later, our motorman pushes a button to throw a switch and our car turns right onto Hayes Avenue. In half a block our double line of track merges to a single track, so the motorman has to set the signal to let any cars heading in our direction know that we have entered the track. A light will turn red way out at the corner of North Depot Street. Out Hayes Avenue we go and, before we know it, we have arrived at the entrance to the Hayes Avenue subway. We are not going to go down in the subway, so our motorman clangs his bell and our track swings right and we make the half-block turn into North Depot Street, even as automobiles must today.

Here we enter a double track that goes the full length of North Depot Street. In a moment we will reach the large railroad depot that is Sandusky's pride. When the Lake Shore and Michigan Southern built the tracks through what was then open fields on the south side of Sandusky, a wooden frame depot typical of the period was erected. But 20 years later, a new depot was built just west of it. It was constructed of

The double tracks of the Depot loop line that enabled two or three streetcars to be waiting when popular afternoon and early evening trains arrived on the New York Central railroad are starting to reappear through the worn pavement on North Depot Street. A ConRail freight train goes by in the background.

Photograph 1988 by Glenn D. Everett

beautiful Amherst buff stone with blue limestone trim. The original frame depot became a freight station and would have still been in use for that purpose as our streetcar rolls by.

The Lake Shore and Michigan Southern had become a subsidiary of the New York Central System and in 1914 lost its corporate identity and its name as it was fully merged into the New York Central Railroad.

Meanwhile, another railroad line had been built which we will find sharing the facilities of the depot. The line, called the Lake Erie and Western, linked Sandusky with Peoria, Illinois. Its founders hoped it would make Sandusky an alternative lake port to the increasingly crowded facilities at Cleveland and Toledo and, at the other end, that Peoria would become an attractive alternative to the crowded rail yards of Chicago. Neither objective was attained.

Although both Sandusky and Peoria prospered, they hardly offered serious rivalry to Cleveland or Chicago.

It was a good try, anyway, and for a number of years the Lake Erie and Western ran both passenger trains and freight trains in and out of Sandusky and to the Illinois Central at Peoria for destinations in the south and west.

We do find our Sandusky depot to be a busy place. As a matter of fact, the Lake Shore Electric Railway used to make it a point to have at least two streetcars at the depot when a popular afternoon train arrived, as one car did not have room enough to carry all the people.

One of these trains has just come in from Cleveland and people are already starting to fill a car standing there ready to go downtown as we come along. Soon a number of people are coming over to board our car, but first some of our passengers jump off and start running to catch that train before it leaves for Toledo. We can hear the conductor calling "All aboard!" but he sees these folks coming and will hold the train a minute for them to climb aboard.

As we wait for the rest of the people to come across the street and board our car, what is that we smell? Fish! Sandusky in those days was the largest fresh water commercial fishing port in the United States, so our Chamber of Commerce boasted in its brochures. Fish caught early in the morning in the nets of fishing boats from the various large fish houses of Sandusky -- Lay Brothers, Booth, Shacht, Post Fisheries and others -- were being loaded aboard the Railway Express car that was carried on the train. The fish arrived at the depot in wooden boxes filled with ice and dripping water as the ice melted.

The fish boxes were loaded on the express cars at the passenger depot, not at the freight station, because the express cars were part of the fast passenger trains. The ice in which the fish were packed had formed in Sandusky Bay the previous winter. As soon as the bay was frozen to a depth of 18 inches or more, the ice harvest immediately began with horses pulling sharp-tipped cutters across the ice. Men followed with long saws to finish cutting the ice into cakes, and then with long poles the ice cakes were propelled through canals of open water cut through the ice to the various fish houses. There a conveyor carried them up to the top of the ice house, from which the heavy cakes slid down into place. The ice houses were built with thick wooden walls filled with sawdust and were so well insulated that the ice was preserved all summer until cracked up and used to pack fish.

Cutting the ice was rugged, cold work and gave rise to the widespread expression of admiration, "He can really cut his ice" or the deprecation, "He just isn't cutting his ice on this job." Well, that's where those sayings came from, and as our streetcar takes aboard passengers at the depot, we watch boxes of fish being loaded aboard the express car. The fish boxes had to be lifted on very fast because the passenger train was on a tight schedule. The fresh fish went right along with the people, and fish caught in Lake Erie early one morning were the next day on the menu of famous restaurants of Chicago and New York City where "Lake Erie perch" and "Lake Erie pickerel" commanded the admiration of gourmet diners.

Yet even while we could watch with fascination as the fish took a ride on the fast train along with the people, the city of Sandusky was dumping all its raw untreated sewage into Sandusky Bay and millions of gallons of raw or partially treated sewage was spewing into Lake Erie from the metropolitan areas of Toledo and Cleveland. Pollution poured down the Detroit River, the Maumee, the Sandusky, the Cuyahoga and many other rivers into the lake with untreated sewage from inland towns. The price has been paid for this abuse. For many years now, not a single commercial fishery has operated in the western end of Lake Erie. A few survive on the Canadian side of the lake where the north shore, devoid of large cities, is less polluted. The job of cleaning up the Great Lakes will continue for many years at great expense.

The annual ice harvest in Sandusky Bay ended in the winter of 1935-36 when the Booth Fisheries building at the foot of Jackson Street by the Municipal Pier was filled for the last time with natural ice. Artificial refrigeration replaced the need for preserving winter ice.

Sandusky's railroad depot is a quiet, nostalgic place now with the only passenger service provided by a couple of Amtrak trains that stop each day to take on a few passengers. In a hostile takeover with the Pennsylvania Railroad, the New York Central Railroad merged as the Penn Central, and then went into bankruptcy. It was taken over by the government-backed Consolidated Railroad Corporation -- or ConRail -- in order to continue operation.

The Lake Erie and Western went bankrupt in the Great Depression of the 1930s, merged with the Nickel Plate, and that line was taken over by the Norfolk and Western, now the Norfolk Southern. The Lake Erie and Western line was abandoned. Remnants of it remain as a silent, rusting memorial to the great era when railroads were America's major transportation system.

There were a lot of interesting things to be seen at the depot. A horse-drawn dray brings up to the freight station a huge casting from the Paper and Textile Machinery Co. -- now the Sandusky Foundry and Machine Co. -- to be placed on a flat car for shipment to a New England textile factory. A little four-cylinder mail truck sputters up to unload several sacks of mail. These will be placed aboard a railway post office car where clerks will sort the mail even as the train moves along, giving faster service, ironically enough, to first-class mail than it ever receives today. Not everything that has happened in the last 60 years has been an improvement.

We also see a big water tank made of wood like a giant barrel 12 feet in diameter 10 feet above the ground on posts, with a large spout. Switch engines would puff up and draw several hundred gallons of water for their tenders. Steam locomotives had to have abundant water to turn into steam, and the water was as essential as the coal that the busy fireman constantly shoveled into the fire beneath the locomotive boiler. The water did not come from the city's water mains but had to be a special mineral-free and chlorine-free water from selected wells along the railroad's right-of-way. It was brought in by tank cars. When the water evaporated as it was turned into steam, the mineral content was left behind and could rapidly encrust and clog the boiler's pipes, leading to frequent and costly cleaning.

Out near Huron there were long troughs in the center of the tracks. Fast trains like the Twentieth Century Limited did not have time to stop and draw water from the railside tanks. Instead, they lowered a scoop and picked up water while going 70 miles an hour or more. There was a loud gushing sound and a lot of spray, but in half a mile the tender of the Limited was filled with water that was scooped up. This was a remarkable sight.

There also was a roundhouse where the locomotives for the Lake Erie and Western could be oiled, greased and repaired and where the fire under their boilers could be started up shortly after midnight so there would be a full head of steam in early morning as the engines pulled out to begin their daily work. The house was literally round so that several engines could come in, each with its own track. There also was a turntable on which they were turned around to face the proper direction. There were dozens of tracks and sidings in the vicinity of the depot so the locomotive could hook up to the proper number of cars to make up a train.

The switch engines hooked up to box cars to take them to the sidings alongside various Sandusky area factories. At the end of the day they brought out to the yards by the depot a couple of dozen cars loaded with products of Sandusky plants ready to go to destinations along the main line.

The depot, quiet although it may be now, was one of the busiest places in the city years ago, and we are sorry that it is time for our streetcar to move along. We have taken on a full load of passengers and several are standing. These are the "straphangers." The gentlemen who have taken seats always gallantly give their seat to any lady who boards, as it was considered most unseemly for any lady to have to reach up and hang onto a strap if there were men seated.

The men also helped the ladies by handing down their suitcases or shopping bags when they got off the car, On the Sandusky streetcars the rules of the Age of Chivalry were always obeyed. Any man who did not help a lady drew frowns of disapproval.

Our car resumes its trip west on North Depot Street even as the train that was at the station starts up. Children always called them "choo-choo" trains because that is just how they sounded as they left the station -- choo, choo, choo, choo! - as the locomotive belched black smoke and steam while its mighty steam pistons drove the huge wheels and the train rapidly accelerated. In fact, the train will almost be out of sight before we reach Camp Street and we will hear its shrill steam whistle sounding the warning as it approaches the distant Mills Street grade crossing.

We have had a great time for a few minutes watching all the things that go on at the depot, but now our car is going to take off. We soon reach Camp Street and angle around the entrance to the Camp Street subway, just as automobiles continue to do today. We enter the center of Camp Street and go down to a single track, setting another warning signal so that we do not meet another car coming toward us head-on.

At West Monroe Street we come to an interesting set of switches. We first go onto a double track for half a block. Then the West Monroe Street car line turns onto our track, but 100 feet later, it must turn off. The two segments of West Monroe Street do not match one another. Today a cut-off has been built that enables automobile drivers to go straight across Camp Street, but in earlier times both automobiles and streetcars had to turn onto Camp Street and then turn off in 100 feet in order to continue out Monroe Street. So there is a great deal of clanking and rattling as we go over this segment of track. We stop to let off some passengers and to pick up people with transfers from the West Monroe line who are now going to ride with us.

We continue along Camp Street until we reach the "Five Points" intersection where we go again onto double track. At this intersection, Camp Street meets Tiffin Avenue, Washington Street and Shelby Street. Shelby is divided into two parts by a narrow park, hence the fifth point. That narrow little park is West Battery Park which never developed into the large recreational park with a swimming pool, marina, tennis courts and restaurant that now mark East Battery Park.

Most people never realize that there is a West Battery Park, but it is a reminder that when Sandusky was laid out in 1818, the War of 1812 had been over for only a short time, and Sandusky's founders were quite worried that the British and Canadian troops across Lake Erie, licking their wounds, might soon try to invade Ohio. They were going to set up batteries of guns at both places to repel them. Nothing more hostile than children's games of cowboys and Indians has ever happened at West Battery, and we can be glad that it is now a symbol of the peace that has endured with Canada for nearly 200 years.

On our streetcar ride, we would have seen another historic monument, now gone, a narrow building between Camp Street and Tiffin Avenue with a little balcony at its northern point. This was where Ohio's Governor William Henry Harrison made a campaign speech to a throng of Sanduskians when running for President in 1840, the election made famous by the slogan "Tippecanoe and Tyler, Too!" The Tippecanooe referred to the battle of Tippecanoe in which General Harrison led a force of militia who put down an Indian uprising. He was also a hero of the Battle of New Orleans which ended the war of 1812.

The Whig Party in its successful campaign for Harrison introduced the innovation of torchlight parades with barrels of hard cider and models of log cabins carried aloft, the first flamboyant American political campaign. We can just see the Whig supporters in Sandusky marching out the dirt road through the woods that was Washington Street, carrying their torches and shouting the slogans. Harrison was elected over old "Fuss and Feathers," as President Martin Van Buren was derisively called, but he lived only one month after his inauguration and was succeeded by Vice President John Tyler who served the remaining three years and 11 months of his term.

The building and its balcony are gone now, despite efforts of Sanduskians to save a very historic landmark. But we used to delight in telling visitors who had just arrived by train of the history of the city. Sandusky still has a lot of history of which to be proud.

As our streetcar turns the corner into West Washington Street, the motorman looks cautiously to the left as the Tiffin Avenue car line joins us at that point. Down the Tiffin Avenue line come not only city streetcars, but all of the interurban cars arriving from Toledo.

We proceed now just two blocks along Washington Street and then turn left onto Lawrence Street. We find that the street ahead is a bit narrow for a double line of tracks. This may have been all right in the days of the horse and buggy, but now there are automobiles parked along both sides, leaving just room for us to pass an interurban car bound for Toledo on the opposite track. One block north at the intersection of Market Street, we see that the two streetcar tracks really do create a problem for the Sandusky Fire Department, whose main station is at the northwest corner of Market and Lawrence Street. The firemen are outside the station practicing with their brand new aerial ladder truck. The truck, which can raise a ladder 85 feet in height, has two operators, the driver in front and a tillerman sitting on a seat perched up on the rear, who turns the rear wheels so that the long truck can make a tighter turn around corners.

The turn is mighty tight to come out of the station, swing left and then turn right into Lawrence Street, and the firemen have complained that they cannot get up the street at any time there is a streetcar on the line. This often delays their response to a fire a critical minute or two.

In the end, the firemen discovered that there is just no way they can get their big new ladder truck up Lawrence Street in a hurry and often the ladder truck, when needed, takes a different route from the pumper truck and the first aid rescue truck.

We continue on Lawrence Street to West Water Street where we turn east toward the downtown section. But first we stop at another railroad station. This is a big brick building on our left which houses the depot of the Big Four Railroad. The Big Four is the Cleveland, Columbus, Cincinnati and St. Louis. Even its initials which appear on the cars, C. C. C. and St. L." are quite a mouthful, so everyone called it the Big Four and, like the Nickel Plate, the nickname stuck, although the railroad never formally adopted it as its corporate name.

The Big Four succeeded the old Mad River and Lake Erie, Sandusky's first railroad. It laid track on a slightly different route, going to Tiffin by way of Castalia and Clyde instead of by way of Bellevue. The original track of the Mad River was laid on wooden rails topped with steel strips. Here and there such a rusty strip will still show up in the fields between Sandusky and Bellevue, marking the last relic of the pioneer line. The Big Four, like the Mad River, ran to Springfield, Ohio, on the banks of Mad River which flows into the Miami River and then the Ohio. Along the way to Springfield, it offered connections with many other railroads, including the main Big Four that linked Cleveland, Indianapolis and St. Louis, which it crossed at Bellefontaine and the other main Big Four line between Toledo and Cincinnati which passed through Springfield.

The Big Four made connections with several other railroad lines that crossed Ohio from east to west, including major junctions at Clyde, Tiffin and Carey. It was an important railroad in its day, and we will pick up more than a dozen passengers who have just arrived on the afternoon train from Springfield.

One block farther on at the intersection of Water and Decatur Streets, we pass yet another depot. This serves the Pennsylvania Railroad, a line that has passenger trains daily to and from Columbus. The evening train from Columbus has not yet arrived, but we do pick up a group of passengers there, ladies who have just finished work at the Catawba Candy Co. They have spent the day at the pleasant task of hand-wrapping the delicious chocolate candy bars this three story brick factory has produced. We see protruding from their purses some candy bars that have been rejected as "imperfects." Sometimes the bars are still quite edible and the workers' families will enjoy them. If not, they will break them into little pieces and put them on the bird feeder. The birds will feast on them. So, too, perhaps will the family dog if the bars don't turn out too gooey. The candy factory which once made thousands of candy bars lost out to the big nation-wide companies that make millions of bars, but it was a great little factory while it lasted.

Now our ride nears its end. We go past the old Biemiller Opera House at the corner of Jackson and Water Streets and see men carrying in pieces of scenery for a live stage production by a touring stock company. We see the same thing at the handsome State Theater at the corner of Columbus Avenue where a live musical stage show will be featured for the weekend. Sandusky had three other downtown motion picture theaters in those days, the Ohio on Market Street, the Plaza on Jackson Street, and the Star on Columbus Avenue.

Our streetcar turns up Columbus Avenue and in a moment we are in front of the interurban station again. We have gone all the way around the loop on the Depot line, and again we can say we have had our eight and one-third cents' worth!

Chapter Five

From East Side to West Side

Get into our "time machine" again and this time we are going to take a ride from the east side to the west side of Sandusky.

We will go out to the East End on the East Monroe Street line and to the West End on the Tiffin Avenue line. The interesting thing about this ride is that we are not going to have to change cars to do it. The same car serves both lines. However, we are going to have to splurge a bit because this is going to take all three of the tokens we get for a quarter. We will get our two bits' worth by the time we are through.

Once again we go down to the interurban station located where Marv Byers' clothing store is now. (Marv gets a lot of free advertising in this book, but that's how it goes when you buy an old interurban station.) Soon a car will come around the corner from West Water Street and the motorman is busy rolling up a new sign in the front window. What will it say? "East Monroe!" Well, that's what we want, so let's hurry up and climb aboard.

We go out and put the first of our three tokens in the farebox and take a seat. The motorman closes the door and off we go up Columbus Avenue, stopping at Market Street and again at Washington Row to take aboard some folks with shopping bags who have been buying groceries and things at the downtown stores. As we pause at West Washington Row, what is that we smell? Popcorn! Yes, the Little Red Wagon was right there where it is now selling fresh popcorn, caramel corn, Cracker Jack and candy. Now if we had pushed the button on our "time machine" to 1934, who would we have seen wearing a white apron and a little round white cap selling the 10-cent sacks of hot popcorn? No one other than the author of this book, holding his first job at the age of 13 at the handsome wage of 50 cents per afternoon (10 cents an hour). Wages were low in those days, but the job was fun. The wagon has been there right where it is now as long as the oldest citizen of Sandusky can remember. We can tell you now the wagon was quite old and had been there a long time already in 1934. We will stop and get some popcorn balls when we have finished our ride. They are only a nickel and a mighty delicious nickel's worth.

At Adams Street some young people get on the car, carrying books they have just borrowed from the Sandusky Public Library. Sandusky was mighty proud then, as now, of its fine public library, the building a gift from Andrew Carnegie, who used his fortune to build scores of such libraries around the nation.

Our car moves on up Columbus Avenue to Monroe Street and there the motorman flicks a button that turns a switch so that we go out East Monroe Street. At Hancock Street where we cross the Soldiers Home/Milan Road Line, several people get on with transfers.

Then we go by the Monroe Street school on our right side and the Sandusky Park Department greenhouse on our left where the beautiful flowers that have so long made our parks famous are grown.

As we near Warren Street, we come to a crossing of the double tracks of the B. & O. Railroad. The railroad's tracks start down at the docks on the waterfront and come right up the center of Warren Street to Madison Street and then start to angle southwestward through Huron Park and cross Monroe Street. The tracks are gone now, but you can still see the right-of-way quite clearly. The line went to Willard, Ohio, where it connected with the B. & O.'s main line between Chicago and Washington, D.C., then went on south to Mansfield and Newark.

The B. & O. trains made a lot of noise as they entered or left Sandusky because they had to blow a warning at every crossing and that meant every block. We don't hear anything, but the motorman has to climb down and look both ways on the tracks to make sure. He hops back on and over the tracks we go with a loud clinking.

At Warren Street we stop again, this time for one of the first red and green stoplights Sandusky had installed to control the growing automobile traffic. We are just getting used to having such lights and more are appearing each year at busy intersections.

When we reach Meigs Street, our double track is going to merge down to a single line since we are going to continue east on First Street which is not wide enough to accommodate two tracks. We wait for a minute until a car coming toward us reaches the double track and safely passes us by. Then, setting the signal to show that we are on the single track portion, we proceed out First Street with the motorman calling out the streets as we go, "Sycamore Line, Anderson Street, McEwen Street," and so on. He pronounces Ogontz Street right. "Oh-Gonts!" he calls out. That street always seems to confuse visitors to the city. They mispronounce that as often as they do Meigs (Meggs) Street. Chief Ogontz was the ruler of the Indian tribe that the earliest settlers found encamped along the bay at Sandusky which in the Indian language meant "Place of Clear Cold Water." Maybe as efforts to clean up Sandusky Bay conuinue, it may again be an appropriate name.

Just after we pass Ogontz Street, we go onto a set of double tracks again. The reason for this is that this car line serves the employees of the East End industrial plants and when the work force begins to go home between 4 p.m. and 6 p.m. a single streetcar cannot hold all the passengers. Two cars have to be at hand. Even though the various plants had learned to stagger their working hours so that not all workers quit at the same time, the many plants -- Farrell-Cheek Foundry, City Ice and Fuel, Jarecki Chemical, Barr Rubber, Holland-Rieger washing machines, and many others -- employed hundreds of persons. Many rode the streetcars to work in the morning and home at night.

At Lane Street, our tracks merge back to a single line and the motorman announces that this is the end of the line. Just ahead of us are many railroad tracks, too many for the streetcar to attempt to cross. One is the track that goes down along the shore of the East Bay, its track on filled land creating the Cove. Others are spur tracks that go into sidings alongside each of the factory buildings. In those days before heavy trucks came into being, railroad cars were the only means of transportation to bring in raw materials or to ship out their finished products. Railroads were utterly essential to the factories' operation.

Streetcars also were essential for transporting workers to and from their work, except for those who lived close enough to the plants to walk.

The streetcar track comes to a dead end just before the many spur tracks begin criss-crossing First Street. All of these tracks have been torn up now, but before they were, it was a rough ride up First Street in an automobile or truck.

Here is the end of the East Monroe streetcar line. Now we are going to see something interesting. Our car is a "double-ender." Such streetcars were common in the old days and it meant they could go in either direction. There is no "forward" or "reverse" as far as an electric motor is concerned. It operates just as well in one direction as the other, depending on which direction the electric current is fed to it.

So when we reach the end of the line, the motorman rolls down his front window. He reaches out to a rope fastened to a trolley that is on that end of the car, unhooks it from a curved metal stanchion that has held it down in place and carefully guides it up until the trolley comes into contact with the overhead wire.

Then he takes a key that locks the front door and disconnects its operating panel, removes the handle with which he controls the car's speed and, with the handle under his arm, walks back the length of the car, flipping the seats as he goes. The backs of the seats are hinged. Thus, by moving the back of the seat from one side to the other, he reverses the direction in which they are facing. We have to get up and let him reverse ours. Then he opens the window on what has been the car's rear end, reaches out for a rope dangling there and pulls the trolley on that end down and secures it under the curved stanchion that will hold it firmly in place. The motorman attaches his operating handle to the panel in front of him, turns a key, adjusts his seat and opens what is now going to be the front door. Presto! Our car has changed direction. What was the front of the car is now the rear and what was the rear is now the front.

The motorman points to the fare box. If we want to ride back into town, we have to drop in another token. He also winds the window sign until the wording "Downtown" appears. We are ready to return to Columbus Avenue and the interurban station.

It is getting near quitting time for the earliest of the factories to let out, so as we go onto the short double track stretch, we find two other city streetcars waiting. They are going to pick up the first of the "rush hour" crowd.

As we reach the double track section again at Meigs Street, we see another eastbound streetcar that has been waiting for us to clear the track. This car, too, is going out to pick up workers coming off the day shift and has a few aboard who are going to work the evening shift.

At the B. & O. Railroad crossing, we wait for a switch engine pushing three or four cars to go past, then we safely cross and we are at Columbus Avenue.

Now we see an ingenious plan the Lake Shore Electric has devised to serve the East End industrial plants. If the car needs to go right back to pick up another load of passengers, it will turn right on Market Street, left on Wayne, left again onto East Water and then turn up Columbus Avenue and he will be all ready to go back to the East End.

However, our car is going to go straight through. When we get to the interurban station, he simply changes his sign to read "Tiffin Avenue" and we pick up some passengers and down Columbus Avenue we go to turn left into West Water Street. Our car serves double duty on the two lines. Out Water Street we go to Lawrence, then left on Lawrence Street. Once again we pass the Central Fire Station. The firemen are all sitting outside in wicker chairs, waiting for the alarm bell to ring. They are having a slow day. Nothing much has happened. But should that alarm bell start ringing, their chairs go flying and they are out of the station on their trucks in a matter of seconds.

We turn on to West Washington Street and our motorman makes certain at "Five Points" that our switch is set to send us out Tiffin Avenue rather than to turn left into Camp Street.

Out Tiffin Avenue we go. At West Monroe Street, we cross that car line. Those passengers who wish to go out West Monroe get off, clutching transfers.

Our car continues on until we reach Broadway Street. Then we move over to the left side and operate on the boulevard. We go under the Tiffin Avenue subway. There are two railroad overpasses over our head. One carries the New York Central tracks, now ConRail. The other carries the Lake Shore and Western which has since been abandoned, but the overpass the railroad built is still there. Did you ever wonder why there are two overpasses there? Oh, you hadn't noticed? Look the next time you go under and you will see.

For years, there has been talk of improving the Tiffin Avenue subway whose warning of only 11 feet clearance is clearly marked. But big interstate trucks no longer go thundering through Sandusky. They take the bypass and any large trucks coming into the city must take caution and choose a different route.

The author well remembers the terrible wreckage that resulted when one large automobile transport truck failed to take heed. All four of the brand new Studebakers on top were reduced to junk. The driver was not hurt, although he presumably had to go to the unemployment office the next day to seek another job. Antique automobile collectors would still shed a tear if they could see all those beautiful 1935 Studebakers being lifted onto a flatbed truck for such salvage as might be possible.

Our streetcar now reaches the end of the Tiffin Avenue line. It would go no farther than Venice Road. The track continues to go on, making a big right turn to operate on the south side of Venice Road. That line is for the interurban cars for Toledo.

Our motorman does his quick double-ender change and points to the farebox where we have to put our third tokens if we want to ride back downtown.

The car moves as quickly as it can down Tiffin Avenue. Behind us, an interurban car is coming up, bound for Cleveland from Toledo by way of Sandusky. The interurban motorman hates to get behind a Sandusky city streetcar that is picking up passengers at several corners as it goes. Even more impatient are the automobile drivers who have to stop and wait respectfully every time the streetcar stops to take on or discharge passengers.

The streetcars were beginning to seriously impede the motor vehicle traffic. This was an ominous sign, especially for the Tiffin Avenue line. It was not producing much revenue since the only large industrial plant it served at the end of its line was the Brightman Nut Co. (now Industrial Nut Corporation). The name "Brightman Nut" always drew a smile from passersby.

Before the days of the Sandusky bypass of Route 2, all through traffic from Toledo to Cleveland had to go along Tiffin Avenue and then through town on Washington Street and Huron Avenue. Traffic was getting heavy and things were getting difficult for the streetcars and interurbans.

Once when the author had been away from Sandusky and lived in Indianapolis for many months, the first sight that greeted our eyes as we entered Sandusky was that of a bright orange streetcar changing the direction of its trolleys at Venice Road and Tiffin Avenue. It was a comforting sight. The orange streetcars were a symbol of Sandusky, a source of civic pride; if the cars were still running, the city was still there.

Symbol of civic pride or not, the Sandusky streetcar system, which made the citizens feel that they lived in a real metropolis, was nearing the end of its day. Every load of new automobiles delivered safely to Sandusky brought the end that much nearer.

Once again, we come around Water Street and turn up Columbus Avenue. We can ride all the way out to the East End again on our token if we want to, but we have already been out there, so let's just ride up to West Washington Row, get off and run over to the Little Red Wagon and get some of those popcorn balls.

Come to think of it, we don't need a "time machine" to do that. The wagon is still there and, when open, still has delicious popcorn. But not for a nickel anymore.

Chapter Six

The Off-Again, On-Again West Monroe Street Line

We still have one more of Sandusky's old streetcar lines to ride. That is, if it is running.

You always had to ask that question about the West Monroe trolley car. The line had never proved profitable for the Lake Shore Electric Railway and was the first in the city to be partially abandoned. Service was discontinued as early as 1928, but this led to protests, especially from the West End industrial plants whose workers it served.

Service was restored, but did not operate at night or on Sunday. Then, in its final days, the line was abandoned from Camp Street to Columbus Avenue and it operated with only a single car shuttling back and forth between Camp Street and Superior Street, which was then the city limit.

So let's step into our "time machine" and go back and take a look and see if we can find the West Monroe trolley car. Zing -- here we go back to the year 1930.

We are in luck, we have picked the right time, for the car is running the full length of the line. So let's hurry down to the interurban station and get our tokens. But we are not going to be able to catch the West Monroe car here. We will ride out Columbus Avenue as far as Monroe Street and get off and wait for a West Monroe car.

Here comes a car marked "East Monroe" now and we will board it. After a ride of six blocks, we ring the buzzer and get off just before the car turns left onto East Monroe Street.

We are going over to the spot just around the corner on West Monroe where we find several other people waiting, most of them with transfers in hand. The West Monroe car is a "double-ender" and its track and trolley wire stops abruptly about 50 feet from the intersection with Columbus Avenue.

51

Why doesn't the West Monroe streetcar simply turn left and go downtown on Columbus Avenue like the East Monroe car does? The answer is that there is already a switch there for the East Monroe car to turn left. It really does not work out to have a double switch at the same point on either a railroad or a streetcar track. It had been tried in various places but resulted frequently in a car "splitting the switch." This could derail a car, damage the switch, and result in an awkward situation when the front wheels of the car went one direction and the rear wheels another.

There also was a problem with the trolley wires overhead. The wires had to touch one another so the little wheel on the top of the trolley could roll along, and there was a flat plate where they met so the trolley could go along in the direction the car was headed and shortly fall into place on the new wire.

This caused trouble once in a while when a car turned east on Monroe Street and the trolley continued going up Columbus Avenue until it fell out of contact. Then the operator of the streetcar had to jump out and go back and put his trolley back on the wire. This is the origin of the common expression, "He's got his wires crossed!" It happened often enough, especially in the earliest days of the streetcars, that people always got a laugh out of it.

The builders of the Sandusky streetcar lines realized that they were inviting trouble if they tried to install a double switch at Monroe Street. If any car split the switch and damaged it at that point, it would not only tie up both the East Monroe and West Monroe streetcar lines, but also the Depot line which passed that point on its way to Hayes Avenue. It would also halt service out Columbus Avenue on the Soldiers Home line and, worst of all, stop interurban traffic from Cleveland to Toledo, as well as to Norwalk. In other words, an accident there would just about tie up the whole system.

Therefore, the West Monroe Street line simply dead-ended near Columbus Avenue and everyone who wished to travel further had to get off and transfer to another car line.

The busy corner at Monroe Street was a frequent source of problems to the streetcar motormen. At any switch there was a "dead spot" on the trolley wire overhead where electric power to the motor was temporarily interrupted. Live power wires cannot touch one another without causing a short circuit, so in turning at a switching point, the trolley encountered a couple of feet of dead wire. In making a turn, the motorman had to get up a little momentum to carry him over the dead spot. The lights inside his car would blink and the power to the motor would stop for a second as he rolled over the switch.

As we stand here at the corner of West Monroe Street waiting for our car, we can watch and see how the motormen on the passing streetcars handle this problem. When they are ready to cross the intersection, as the Soldiers Home and Depot cars do, they ring their bells and start up quickly, then roll over the switch and, their power, cut off for a second, returns and on they go. The East Monroe car motorman carefully waits for any traffic ahead of him, then rings his bell vigorously, and starts up as fast as he can so that his car turns and rolls past the dead spot and resumes power as the trolley, with a shower of sparks, comes in contact with the new line going out East Monroe.

Maybe we will see something really interesting happen. This author was on an East Monroe car one time when the motorman had to jam his brakes in going over the switch. A careless boy on his bicycle had ignored the ringing of the bell and had pedaled out across Monroe Street right in front of the turning car. The motorman, with a loud mutter, had to jam on his brakes to avoid striking him. Sure enough, the car was caught underneath the dead spot on the trolley wire.

The motorman tried as hard as he could, but simply was unable to maneuver his trolley into contact with the live part of the wire ahead. He had to get back on and ask half a dozen men and boys if they would help push the car a foot or two. We got down the steps and ran to the back. An empty car was light enough and moved with so little friction on the rails that a couple of men probably could have pushed it forward, but a car loaded with passengers was another matter. Push as we would, the car would not budge. The motorman had to go forward and ask the fat lady sitting in front if she would mind getting off for just a moment. She obliged, with a laugh, and a woman holding a child followed her. With the car then more than 400 pounds lighter, we managed to move it around the curve in the track onto East Monroe

Street. The trolley sparked and crackled as it came into contact with the live wire, lights came on again in the car and the fat lady eased herself back up the steps with everyone else following.

Occasionally, a streetcar would get into more serious problems at a switch and would get off the rails.

The Lake Shore Electric had a big work car at its car barn for such difficulties. The work car carried big heavy-duty jacks that could lift the disabled car right up and set it over on the tracks. However, it required a little time to get the work car to the scene.

Streetcar maintenance men were very good at getting derailed cars back on the track, just as are railroad crews now. In fact, railroads today, due to poor maintenance, seem to be having more derailments than ever before. Today many trains carry toxic chemicals and hundreds of people have to be evacuated from their homes whenever a derailment occurs.

Streetcar's did not jump the tracks often but it was a very interesting spectacle when they did. One time a Depot Line car heading south on Camp Street was struck by a truck carelessly backing out of a driveway on the left side of the street. The truck bumped the front of the streetcar and it went off the rails at a 45 degree angle and up over the curb on the right. The car certainly looked ridiculous in that position and everybody in the neighborhood seemed to have come out to look at it. The work car arrived and with a great deal of tugging and squealing of metal, the car was pulled back onto its track. The motorman climbed on and tentatively checked the power. The car moved ahead and there was a loud cheer from the spectators.

As we stand at the corner of Columbus Avenue and Monroe Street today, everything seems to be going smoothly. A streetcar heading out to the Soldiers Home goes up Columbus Avenue and one coming from the Soldiers Home comes down the other side. A car coming from the Depot turns onto the Columbus Avenue track from Hayes Avenue and goes by with a clatter. Then a car turns off East Monroe to head downtown. Finally, here comes a big interurban car for Cleveland, heading up the avenue. You can see how a streetcar switch took quite a beating, particularly with automobiles and an occasional horse-drawn wagon passing over it, too. Streetcar tracks required constant repair because of the punishment they took.

Several cars have gone by on Columbus Avenue, but where is the West Monroe Street car? That was a question you often had to ask. Out in the West End it had to cross the tracks that took both Big Four and Pennsylvania trains out of Sandusky. The Pennsylvania brought hundreds of cars full of coal to the Lower Lake docks to be loaded onto the big lake boats. These vessels brought iron ore from Minnesota to Cleveland or Lorain to feed the furnaces of the huge steel mills, then they came to Sandusky and took cargoes of coal back.

Sometimes it took 10 minutes or longer for a coal train to pass over the Monroe Street grade crossing. This delayed the streetcar line. The West Monroe line consisted of a single track except for a short double track at the intersection with Camp Street which enabled the two cars that operated on the line to pass one another. Thus, if one car was held up at the railroad crossing, inevitably the other one was delayed too, for it had to wait at Camp Street for the arrival of the other.

Another problem that plagued the West Monroe Street line was the mischievous boys who lived in the neighborhood through which it passed. They delighted in dashing out from between parked cars and pulling on the rope that was connected to the trolley, making it jump off the wire and cutting off the power to the streetcar's motor. The motorman, shaking his fist, would have to climb down when his car rolled to a stop and walk back and put his trolley back in contact with the wire.

Often, no sooner had he gone back to the front and started the car again than -- zing! -- his trolley was off the wire again.

"We finally worked out a deal with him," says Frank LaGrass, now a respected senior citizen of Sandusky. "If he would let us ride, we would stand in the rear and make sure nobody took his trolley off the wire."

One can just see Frankie and his pals leaning out the back window on their elbows, and great misfortune was sure to befall anyone who tried to touch the trolley while it was under their protection.

"We never paid a fare on the West Monroe car," he recalls with a smile, "and the motorman was glad for our company on the ride."

LaGrass also remembers how on bitter winter mornings when the wind was sweeping across the frozen ice of Sandusky Bay and snow was in the air, the operator would see the little six and seven-year-old children struggling along the icy sidewalk toward their class at Barker Elementary school and Holy Angels school and would stop the car and shout, "Come on, kids, climb on and I'll give you a ride to school!"

Father Armitage may not have been able to make holy angels out of all his students in the West End neighborhood, but they were all grateful for the streetcar line even if they usually had to ride it free against company rules.

Finally, we see the West Monroe car coming toward us. We will not criticize the motorman, for it is not his fault the car is late. He is doing his best. A dozen passengers get off the car as it comes to stop at the end of its track. They are clutching transfers and hurry across Columbus Avenue to catch a streetcar heading downtown.

The motorman quickly changes his trolleys, reverses the seats in the car and, in a moment, opens the front door that was formerly the rear door. All the people who have gathered on the corner with us quickly climb aboard.

We notice, as we do so, that not only do we hand him transfers, but so do all the other people. This was one of the troubles with the West Monroe line. On its way out Monroe Street to the west, it collected largely transfers from other lines. On the way back down toward town, nearly every passenger wanted a transfer to continue on another line. Very few people rode it just to go from one place on West Monroe Street to another. The line was never a money-maker.

Our car is ready to take off and our motorman will do his best to get back on the 15-minute schedule the line is supposed to keep. As we roll along West Monroe Street, let's wave at the teams playing softball on the diamond in Central Park at the corner of Fulton Street and at the children on the swings, slides and merry-go-round in the playpark across the way.

As we move along, the motorman calls out the streets in a happy sing-song voice. "Fulton Street," he cries, "Maple

Avenue, Central Avenue, Vine Street, Stone Street!" Soon he calls out "A Street!" Sure it's a street. What street? "'A' Street!" Well, if so, where is "B" Street? Strangers in town would always wonder about that. There was no ready answer, for Sandusky's streets are not always very logical in their names. "A" Street was there all by itself. There was no "B" Street. And soon we are at Camp Street where, as we make our complicated turn onto the Camp Street car line and then off it again, we see the other West Monroe trolley car waiting for us to pass. As soon as we do, the motorman of that car takes off for Columbus Avenue.

We enter a single track section again. Soon our motorman calls out "J Street!" "J?" Where is the rest of the alphabet? No; it is "Jay Street" named for John Jay, the early American patriot and our first Chief Justice of the United States Supreme Court.

Then we are at Tiffin Avenue where a number of passengers get on handing the motorman transfers from the Tiffin Avenue line. We are off again and the motorman calls out "Broadway!" We take a look at that street which has hardly lived up to its name, a side street only three blocks long. Then we are at King Street. King? Surely not named for King George III but, if we will take a look down its two-block length, as some sailors get off our streetcar to return to their big lake boat moored at the coal loading docks there at the foot of King Street, we will see a remarkable sight. The huge coal loading machine is lifting up an entire railroad gondola car and, grasping it with giant claws, tips it upside down as the coal roars down a chute into the hold of the seamen's boat which is nearly ready to take off for its voyage up the Great Lakes with a full cargo of coal. Visitors to Sandusky used to watch this mechanical marvel with awe and admiration.

Now we reach the first of our railroad crossings. We go over the single track of the Big Four. Although this track was abandoned later in the 1930s when the Big Four merged into the New York Central System, it remained in place for four decades before being torn up. The Big Four station on Water Street was torn down and thereafter its two daily passenger trains were operated from the New York Central depot. Patrons of the old Toft's Dairy bar used to park nervously on the track that ran through its parking lot because it always looked as though the track was still in operation.

In the 1930s the track was still in use and our motorman had to be careful in crossing it, for it did not offer a good view. Trains almost came to a stop as they crossed Monroe Street. But now our streetcar approaches the double tracks of the Pennsylvania Railroad (today operated by the Norfolk Southern) and here our motorman does not have to dismount and look both ways. There is a watchman on duty who is either sitting in a little shed by the side of the tracks or is out in the middle of the street holding up a large sign that says "STOP." Switch engines were always busy moving coal cars either toward the coal loading docks or taking empty cars away and automatic signals would have been blinking needlessly all the time. When a locomotive engineer was actually ready to take a string of cars across Monroe Street, he would signal the watchman who would immediately stop traffic.

The watchman today waves us on and we pitch and sway in our seats as our streetcar crosses the tracks. Before long, we find ourselves at Superior Street where the car track ends abruptly precisely at the western corportion limit of the city of Sandusky. The city in those days had not yet annexed the Venice area.

Here our motorman calls out, "End of the line, folks!" and begins to switch his trolleys so his "double-ender" can reverse its direction. If we want to go back, we must drop another token in the farebox. Since it is a long walk back to Columbus Avenue, we quickly do so and take our place on the now-reversed seats.

Several young people climb aboard our car. They have been enjoying a happy day swimming at Winnebago Park. The park, then called Lions Park because the Sandusky Lions Club gave the park to the city, had a fine little beach created by dumping a number of truck loads of sand on the shore of the bay at that point. It was a favorite swimming place in summer and many children rode the West Monroe Street streetcar to reach it.

Today it may be just as difficult to imagine Sandusky Bay as a body of water in which it was pleasant and safe to swim as it is to visualize the little streetcars that brought them to this spot near the park. Pollution has taken its toll. A strong fence along the shoreline ensures that no one goes swimming there now. Many of the children simply wear their bathing suits under their skirts or shorts and you have to be careful of wet seats on the West Monroe car on warm days because they don't always sit on their towels.

The motorman rings his bell, closes the door, and off we go back toward town. We again cross the railroad tracks safely and reach Camp Street where we pass the other car on the line and let off some of our passengers who are going to take the Depot line. Before we know it, we are back at Columbus Avenue, where we run across the street to get on a car coming from the direction of the Soldiers Home to present our transfers and complete our ride downtown.

We have enjoyed a ride on the West Monroe line but as we watch the motorman again reversing his trolleys, we cannot help but wonder how much longer that streetcar line is going to be there for people to ride?

The Trolley Car Era was a great one but it was going to be a short one. Many older people at that time in Sandusky who well remembered the excitement and anticipation with which they watched the tracks being laid for a fine new system of electric cars were soon going to see the tracks rusting and eventually covered over with asphalt paving. Before long, it will only be with the "time machine" provided by memory that we will be able to ride the West Monroe Street line any more.

Tall as a soldier stands this pole on Milan Road at the corner of the fence surrounding the Ohio Veterans Home. Note that when it is necessary to replace one of the poles put in place nearly a century ago or to repair it because of a lightning strike, the utility company has to splice two regular size poles together to match the old poles in height. It is hard to find trees that tall from which to make such poles now.

Photograph 1988 by Glenn D. Everett

Chapter Seven

A Fast Ride on the Big Interurban

We have taken a ride on all the old Sandusky streetcar lines. But the city streets rumble daily to the sound of the big interurban cars which operate east to Cleveland, west to Toledo and south to Norwalk.

So before we come to the end of our story, let's take a ride on the interurbans and see where they go. We go to the interurban station on downtown Columbus Avenue where we find 30 or 40 people sitting on the benches waiting for the Limited for Cleveland. We buy a round-trip ticket for Cleveland which will cost us about $2.50.

The Limited will stop only at Soldiers Home, Huron, Vermilion, Ceylon Junction, Mitiwanga, Lorain, Rocky River and Lakewood before it rolls onto the north side of Public Square in Cleveland which is its ultimate destination.

There we will find other interurban cars that go to Akron, Canton, Youngstown and Ashtabula, for in the 1920s the interurban lines fanned out in all directions from major cities.

If we were to wait for the later and much slower-moving "local," we would find that it would stop a dozen times before we even reach Huron and between Huron and Vermilion it would stop at Old Homestead, Anderson Acres, Ruggles Beach, Beulah Beach, and nearly 20 other places designated as "stops" for the local riders.

The ticket clerk behind the desk receives a signal that has been flipped by the interurban motorman as he rounds the corner of Lawrence and Water Streets.

"Toledo car now arriving!" he calls out. "Passengers for Cleveland, Lorain and Ceylon Junction all aboard please!"

"This is the car for Cleveland," he repeats. "All aboard!"

Long before smoking and non-smoking sections became mandatory on
public transportation, the Lake Shore Electric divided its interurban cars with
a glass partition and sliding glass door. The smoking section (foreground)
had leather seats and a linoleum floor. The non-smoking area had plush-
covered seats with linen-draped headrests and a carpeted floor and footrests.

We hasten out the station door, for the car will stop for
only a minute. As soon as we reach the curb, we see the big
orange car rounding the corner from Water Street onto Columbus Avenue. The interurban cars are much larger than the
city streetcars. Nearly 100 people can ride on one. We board
at the rear steps, but, as we cluster around, the passengers
getting off at Sandusky come down, many clutching satchels
and packages. We climb up now and discover that the interurban has a two-man crew. The conductor, resplendent in a
blue uniform with brass buttons, rides in the back, while
the motorman is in his own cubicle at the front, separated
from the passengers.

The conductor asks our destination as we climb aboard. He
has to make certain everyone is catching the right car. When
we tell him "Cleveland," he waves us into the car where we

A typical Lake Shore Electric Railway interurban car photographed about 1915. These cars were supplemented later with some even larger. Note the compressed air tanks underneath which operated the brakes.

find that we are going to have nice big plush seats and will be able to ride in much more comfort than on the wooden seats in our little city streetcars. We are also quite a bit higher above the tracks and will have a great view.

We find, too, that the interurban had a "smoking section" on its cars long before it became popular to have smoking and non-smoking sections. The "smoker" was in the forward part of the car and separated from the rest by a varnished wooden door with a big brass knob and a glass partition so you could look through it. Gentlemen who wanted to smoke the big and very odorous cigars that were popular then or who chewed tobacco took seats in the "smoker." Women never smoked in public in those days. The "smoker" had leather seats, rather than plush-covered and a linoleum floor instead of carpet. It also had big brass spitoons that they hoped the tobacco chewers would hit when they spit out their cud. Few men smoked cigarettes in those days.

The moment everyone has come up the steps, our conductor gives two sharp tugs on a cord which rings a bell up front to tell the motorman to proceed. The conductor suddenly gives one tug and the motorman stops. A man comes running and jumps aboard. He has almost missed the car. The conductor gives two pulls and we are off again. Anyone else will have to wait an hour for the next interurban.

We roll up Columbus Avenue. Soon we are leaving the center of Columbus Avenue and roll along on the east boulevard north of Scott Street. As we cross the New York Central and B. & O. tracks, we look down at the big excavation they are digging for what will be the new Columbus Avenue subway. It is a remarkable engineering project as they keep the train traffic moving while they build the subway underneath it.

At the corner of Perkins Avenue, we wait for a city streetcar to pass us in the opposite direction. As we do so, we hear a loud whirring underneath our car. Every time an interurban car stops, we hear this noise. It is the air compressor motor raising the pressure in the air tanks so we will have plenty of air to apply the brakes. Interurbans travel fast out in the country and the motorman has a dial that shows him the pressure in the tank. It takes a lot of braking power to stop one of these big cars.

The air compressor motor draws too much electricity to operate while the car is in motion, so almost every time we come to a stop, it automatically turns on and the loud whining noise it makes is one of the first things you notice about interurban cars. The whole car vibrates while it runs. From time to time, if air pressure gets too low, the motorman will remain at a stop for a moment or two, letting it re-charge. Everyone looks out to see where the latecomer is for whom the interurban seems to be waiting, but they see no one. We are just re-charging the air tank. In a moment the compressor shuts off and down the track we go.

When the city streetcar has safely passed us on the other track, we move off onto a single track on the east side of Columbus Avenue and we get a beautiful view now of the car barns from our high seat on the interurban. We can see all the way back to where the old antique cars are stored. The old wooden cars of the 1890s already look very strange and old-fashioned in the 1920s. As we pass the Erie County Infirmary, we wave to a couple of the elderly gentlemen who sit on a sunny bench and wave a friendly greeting to the passing interurbans. Before we know it, we have reached the Soldiers Home station.

We stop only a moment at the busy station there. An interurban bound in the opposite direction pulls out as we pull in. We pause while a couple of passengers get off and two or three others get on and then we take off down the track that runs alongside the Soldiers Home fence. As we look over the fence, we see the cottages where the veterans live. At Milan Road we turn right and go along the west end of the road. As we pass the Wagner quarry, opposite what is now the big Sandusky shopping mall, we pass some big piles of dirt and gravel, 30 or 40 feet high, soil that had been stripped off to uncover the fine limestone that has been quarried there for nearly a century. The piles largely disappeared when they were used to supply fill for construction of the Ohio Turnpike in 1954 and later the Route 2 bypass south of Sandusky. But in the 1920s these "artificial mountains" were very awesome as the interurban cars passed beside them.

At the corner of Hull Road, we reach a switch. Our motorman flips the switch so that we turn left, cross Milan Road and proceed on the track that is on the south side of Hull Road. Had we gone straight ahead, we would have remained on a track that carried interurban cars to Norwalk. It stayed on the west side of Milan Road to Avery where it crossed the tracks of what was then the Nickel Plate Railroad.

The tracks changed sides of the road at the intersection of Huron-Avery Road and went down into the Milan River valley. There they crossed the tracks of the Wheeling and Lake Erie Railroad that went along the Huron River banks to Huron to carry cargo to and from the coal and iron ore docks in Huron harbor. The line, as it climbed Milan Hill, passed within sight of the little brick home that was the birthplace of Thomas A. Edison.

The track went around Milan town square and then south to Norwalk where it connected with an interurban line that went to Monroeville, Bellevue, Clyde and Fremont, with connections to many other cities.

However, we are going toward Cleveland, so we now are passing the farms of Perkins Township as we roll along Hull Road. At this point the conductor comes along to collect the tickets of passengers who boarded in Sandusky and at Soldiers Home. He punches and tears off the first portion of our round-trip ticket; in a slot above our heads he puts the stub which tells him our destination. If we should fall asleep, he will come and wake us up before we reach our stop. We are not in any danger of falling asleep, however, on this trip.

At Galloway Road, we cross to the north side of Hull Road. If we look to our left we will see the newly-completed clubhouse of the Plum Brook Country Club. Some of the old-timers aboard our car will still shake their heads and ask why all this fine farmland had been turned into grassy slopes just so some players could hit little white balls toward holes marked by flags. We will have to duck if one of the duffers on the course slices a ball toward us.

Let's keep our heads up, though, for the most exciting part of our trip is about to come. As we approach the point where Hull Road is going to cross the tracks of the New York Central Railroad and join the Cleveland Road, or Lake Road as it was called then, we start climbing up a man-made hill

One of the vestiges of the Lake Shore Electric line still visible after half a century is the abutment that carried the trestle across the main line of the New York Central (now ConRail) at Slate Cut where Hull Road intersects the Lake Road five miles east of Sandusky.

Photograph 1988 by Glenn D. Everett

and we cross the railroad tracks safely on a high steel trestle bridge. It is rather scary, though. The trestle is narrow, just wide enough for our car and as we look down it seems as though we are going through thin air because we cannot see the track that is supporting us. And down below a fast train is approaching, with smoke belching from its locomotive and its steam whistle blowing a warning for the Hull Road grade crossing and the Camp Road crossing, both of which are below us.

The stop which we make as we descend from our high ride over the tracks is called Slate Cut. The name originated because, when the railroad was built, they had to cut through a lot of slate rock to make the line level.

"Slate Cut!" cries out the conductor and a couple of passengers get up to leave. They have to step lively down the rear steps because the interurban is only going to pause for a moment and the conductor sounds two sharp rings of his bell as they leave the last step. Off we go!

An exciting point on the interurban line to Cleveland was the high trestle which carried Lake Shore Electric cars over the busy main line of the New York Central railroad at Slate Cut between Sandusky and Huron.

Hayes Presidential Center
Charles E. Frohman Collection

We stop again for a brief moment as the conductor cries out "Rye Beach!" The Rye Beach Road was just a narrow little country road that intersected the Lake Road by a little brick one-room schoolhouse that had recently been converted to a house as a result of abandonment of the tiny one-room schools. Children along here now rode the interurban to school either at Sandusky or Huron as a result of school consolidation.

In the earliest days, the interurban track followed the south side of the Lake Road all the way to Huron, but then the so-called Huron Cut-off was built to shorten time between Sandusky and Cleveland. So we now go straight off in the midst of open fields, making a beeline for Huron. At this point, the motorman pushes his throttle up to full speed and we roll along at 70 miles an hour or more.

The first thing we know we are at the station in Huron. Here more people get on and off. The conductor tosses off a bundle of newspapers to a waiting paperboy. The interurbans were frequently used to speed newspaper deliveries to outlying communities.

Now another exciting point has arrived as we cross the Huron River and then we roll along the south side of the Lake Road with the conductor calling out "Old Homestead Beach!" "Ruggles Beach!" and so on, as we move along, pausing only briefly at each point a passenger is waiting.

Now the conductor calls out "Ceylon Junction!" A dozen people get up and prepare to leave. There is a large interurban station at Ceylon, a little place that otherwise has only a couple of greenhouses, half a dozen houses and a small store.

But this is a major junction for the interurban line. Here we connect with the line that goes south to Norwalk by way of Berlin Heights and goes on through Monroeville, Clyde, Bellevue and Fremont where there are also connections to other cities.

A considerable number of people get on and then we are off again until we arrive in Vermilion. From there we pass over the Vermilion River and go on to Lorain where there is a big interurban station and a connection with electric cars going to Elyria and other points south.

We are going to cross the Black River, but we have to wait until the drawbridge comes down. It has just allowed a big lake iron ore freighter to pass.

From Lorain we go on to Rocky River where we cross a deep gorge and then we are going along the boulevard past the lawns of beautiful new homes in the then-growing Cleveland suburb of Lakewood.

Finally we reach the city limit of Cleveland and we find ourselves moving out in the center of busy Detroit Avenue and we cross the Cuyahoga River on yet one more exciting high bridge and come at last to Cleveland's busy Public Square.

The Public Square in those days was the hub of a large city streetcar system. The long cars were almost as long as our own big interurban car but not quite as high. Our conductor announces that this is the end of the line and we get off as he gives directions to other passengers who are going to catch interurban cars south to Akron or Canton or eastbound for Euclid, Willoughby, Mentor, Painesville and Ashtabula.

We are going to enjoy ourselves shopping in the big Higbee Store and the May Company store right there facing Public Square and then catch an interurban home for the two-hour ride back to Sandusky.

So that was the ride to Cleveland. Now on another day we can take an interurban the other direction from Sandusky to Toledo. That car will approach the interurban station in Sandusky, of course, going north toward the Bay.

The man behind the counter will call out, "Car for Castalia, Fremont, Genoa, Woodville and Toledo with connections for Detroit, Wauseon, Bryan, Fort Wayne and points west!"

The Toledo car will turn left on Water Street after it leaves Columbus Avenue. It will stop at the Pennsylvania Railroad Depot at Decatur Street and the Big Four Depot, just beyond Fulton Street, to pick up additional passengers; then it will turn left up Lawrence Street. We will watch apprehensively as we pass the Central Fire Station but the firemen are sitting in the sun, waiting for the fire alarm bell to ring. Fortunately it is a quiet day for them. At Washington Street we turn right and at Tiffin Avenue we angle left and go on to the point at Broadway Street, a little beyond Monroe Street, where we will turn left onto the boulevard to go under the railroad overpasses. At Venice Road, we turn right and go along the south side of the road until we reach the Pennsylvania Railroad tracks which go to

69

the coal docks. We pass that point very slowly and carefully and then we turn left.

To our right is the track of the Big Four railroad going south to Clyde, Tiffin, Bellefontaine and Springfield. Just beyond is the track of the Lake Erie and Western going to Fremont, via Vickery, and then on west to its eventual terminal in Peoria, Illinois.

There are three separate sets of tracks. Each has its own independent roadbed, with deep ditches between the three sets of tracks. Our motorman opens his throttle and soon we are going 70 miles an hour or faster. As we approach Homegardner Road, he sounds his loud air horn. When the early-day motorists heard the air horn of an approaching interurban, they knew better than to try to race it to the crossing. The interurban would go by as an orange flash! Many times it seemed from the rush of wind the car stirred that it must be going 100 miles an hour. Historians claim it was only about 70, but it often looked faster than that.

Before we knew it, in about four minutes, we are slowing down for Castalia.

The village of Castalia had a big station in those days, for with the interurban cars coming every half hour in one direction or the other and with several passengers trains a day in each direction on the two railroads, Castalia was a busy place. Today it seems impossible that this station and all the tracks have disappeared. Out in the countryside, however, you can still find traces of where the rights-of-way were before the tracks were torn up.

From Castalia, our track aims straight as an arrow across open fields in the direction of Fremont, rather than going alongside a road. We slow as we cross a railroad spur that goes to the Castalia quarry a mile south of us and then as we cross over the main line of the Big Four. We also cross a unique little narrow gauge rail line which carries small hopper cars loaded with marl, a type of clay that is used in the manufacture of Portland cement. The little line carries the material from the marl beds near Castalia to a big cement plant at Bay Bridge. The cute little steam engine looks as though it was meant for an amusement park but this line is strictly for business.

We make one stop at the tiny hamlet of Erlin. Little is left of that village now but if we pass it today on State

70

Route 412, we can see a row of interurban poles that mark the old interurban line. The tracks were pulled up but since the poles were also used to carry electric power wires that serve that area, they were left in place and have long survived the big orange cars whose trolley wire they carried.

We reach Fremont in only a few minutes where our car moves out into the center of the street and then crosses the Sandusky River on a long bridge. The station is just across the bridge and serves as a railroad depot as well as an interurban station, as a railroad track runs right alongside the west bank of the Sandusky River at that point.

From Fremont we will go, alternately alongside a road and then across open fields, stopping in the towns of Genoa and Woodville, until in an hour we find ourselves on the city streets of Toledo and crossing the broad Maumee River on the Cherry Street Bridge to the interurban station in downtown Toledo. Here we will find many other interurban lines that will go to Detroit with connections to Michigan points; Fort

Looking east on State Route 412 in the now almost vanished hamlet of Erlin, the stately line of interurban poles can be seen as they carried the interurban trolley wire through Erlin and across the fields beyond. A track no longer runs beneath the poles but across field and valley they still carry electric power lines to serve the rural area.

Photograph 1988 by Glenn D. Everett

71

Wayne with connections to Indiana cities; and west to Wauseon and Bryan. Toledo was the hub of interurban lines that linked it to many cities.

We plan to spend our day at the Toledo Zoo, one of the largest and best in the country. It used to be quite an adventure to take the interurban to Toledo for a visit to the zoo. This author well remembers getting a ride on the back of the zoo's favorite tame elephant. Riding an elephant is an even bigger thrill than riding the big interurban car! Get your dime ready and get in line for a ticket. We can have quite a day at the zoo and then we go back to the interurban station on one of the big Toledo city streetcars to take our one hour and 50 minute ride back to Sandusky.

That is how it was when you could ride the big interurban cars.

Chapter Eight

1932: The Beginning of the End

The Lake Shore Electric line began to face difficult days after 1929. The great stock market crash of October, 1929, triggered an economic depression that grew steadily worse month by month. Banks failed and many businesses went into bankruptcy. In those days, there was no such thing as unemployment insurance and no federal insurance of bank deposits. When a bank suddenly closed, depositors lost all their money. Only after months of liquidation did they stand a chance of getting any of it back and then usually only a small part. When an industrial plant or a retail store closed its doors, all of the employees were out of work and they did not have a dollar of income until they could find another job. Unemployment was widespread and jobs of any kind were hard to find. There was no Social Security and elderly people who lost their life savings in bank failures or the collapse of the stock market were in poverty.

Patronage on both the city streetcar lines and the interurbans steadily declined. This accentuated a trend that had already started in the 1920s as the increasing number of automobiles and the expansion of paved highways that replaced dirt roads encouraged more people to use cars for trips rather than rely on public transportation.

Motor buses were beginning to appear which, like automobiles, were larger, had more powerful motors, and were beginning to operate between cities on the newly-paved highways. These buses did not require the maintenance of expensive tracks, bridges, trolley wires, switches and other equipment needed by electric railways. With lower costs and more flexibility of routes, the buses were rapidly becoming very competitive.

The great interurban era reached its peak in 1907, according to railway historians, when one enterprising traveler figured out a way to go from Boston to Chicago and as far west as the Mississippi River entirely on electric railways, changing interurban lines over 30 times, but covering only 1,500 miles. There were optimistic forecasts that it soon would be possible to go all the way from coast to coast on interurban cars. But it was not to be. The era of rapid expansion ended, and those lines which really were not economically successful from the start began first to consolidate and then, mile by mile, to abandon some of the trackage that had been so enthusiastically constructed.

As early as 1922, whole lines began to disappear, victims of the rising competition of buses and automobiles and of high maintenance costs of their systems of tracks. When the Great Depression struck, electric railways, already in weak financial condition, began to go into bankruptcy in mounting numbers.

Railroads began to collapse into bankruptcy, too, and the number of passenger trains rapidly dwindled. The railroads were soon to face competition from another source, particularly for their lucrative Pullman sleeping car trains that operated overnight between major cities and on three-day schedules across the country. Airplanes were beginning to carry passengers and within a few years, passengers were flying from New York to Los Angeles in a few hours instead of taking $3\frac{1}{2}$ to 4 days on a train.

In the city of Sandusky, its excellent network of streetcar lines began to feel the pressure, as did the interurban service that linked it to Cleveland, Toledo, and other cities. In a desperate effort to raise flagging revenue, the fare on city streetcars was raised to 15 cents a ride or four tokens for 50 cents. This was much more expensive than the three-for-a-quarter rate of the 1920s. It encouraged people to walk instead of paying $12\frac{1}{2}$ cents per ride. After all, we have to remember how low wages were during the Depression. When Congress established the first minimum wage law for interstate commerce in 1937, it was only 25 cents an hour. A streetcar token cost half and hour's pay at the minimum wage.

A lot of jobs did not pay even 25 cents an hour in the Depression. Service industries, like restaurants and summer resorts were exempt from the law. This author in 1939 worked an entire summer at Cedar Point on a 10-hour-a-day, 7-day-a-week job, that paid 18 cents an hour. Anyone who made as much as 50 cents an hour had a plush job. It is understandable in such economic conditions why streetcar patronage fell off and why fewer people took trips to Cleveland or Toledo on the interurbans unless on urgent missions.

The West Monroe Street carline was the first to go. It was discontinued, then resumed, and then was shortened to one car that shuttled back and forth from Camp Street out to Superior Street.

A decision by the city of Sandusky to repave West Washington Street in 1932 brought about a crisis. A double streetcar track ran down the center of the street from the Five Points intersection with Tiffin Avenue two blocks to Lawrence Street. The street was in such poor condition from the heavy traffic it carried that a complete repaving job all the way down to its base was deemed absolutely necessary. What were they going to do about reconstructing and repaving the car tracks that were in the middle of the street?

This same problem of street repaving was facing the remaining streetcar systems all over the nation. It is relatively simple to put down a new coat of asphalt. We have all seen streets being prepared for this with manholes raised an inch or so and sometimes gutters and curbs repaired and raised along the sides of streets before the new layer of paving is applied. But when there are streetcar tracks in the middle of the street, it is a major task to reconstruct the whole trackbed and replace the rails. It is much simpler to just cover up the rails with the new layer of paving.

The Lake Shore decided to abandon its Washington Street tracks. This also meant abandoning the entire Tiffin Avenue line. It, too, was threatened by repaving, for Tiffin Avenue was becoming filled with potholes.

In the days before the Sandusky bypass was built from the new Sandusky Bay bridge east to Huron, all the automobile and truck traffic between Toledo and Cleveland on State Route 2 had to enter Sandusky at Venice Road, go down Tiffin Avenue, to Washington Street, through the center of town, out Huron Avenue, to Warren Street and eventually to Cleveland Road. The heavy volume of traffic was tearing up

Sandusky streets along its route. This also was the route taken by U.S. 6 through the city.

The repaving of Washington Street brought about the final demise of the Tiffin Avenue line and meant that the loop line around the Depot would have to be shortened to a line that dead-ended at the corner of Camp Street and Washington Street. There the double-ender trolley car would reverse its trolleys and its direction, then simply go back up Camp Street, across North Depot Street and down Hayes Avenue instead of continuing around the loop.

Along with the Tiffin Avenue tracks the Lake Shore was abandoning its two tracks on Lawrence Street to the relief of the Sandusky Fire Department which had recently acquired an aerial ladder truck that could not negotiate Lawrence Street successfully when there was a city streetcar or interurban car in the way. The firemen had taken to driving the ladder truck down Market Street to Decatur Street to get out to many alarms in the city or, for a fire in the West End, to go all the way to Pearl Street and then up to Tiffin Avenue.

Further, the Lake Shore was abandoning its dual tracks on Water Street from Columbus Avenue to Lawrence Street. This portion of the system was no longer profitable either. The same Depression which was bringing financial ruin to the interurban system was also bankrupting the railroads. The Big Four railroad went out of business, selling its tracks to the New York Central. Soon thereafter the wrecking ball fell on the large Big Four passenger station at the corner of Water Street and Lawrence. The two daily trains the Big Four continued operating to Springfield were powered now by one of the first diesel units seen in northern Ohio, instead of a steam engine.

The chug-chug of the exhaust pipes on the "doodlebug," as Sanduskians soon dubbed the two-car diesel-powered passenger train, could be heard every morning as it warmed up out at the New York Central station on North Depot Street. The "doodlebug" lasted only seven years. It went into oblivion in 1937 as all passenger service was discontinued on the former Big Four.

At the same time, the Pennsylvania Railroad discontinued its daily train from Sandusky to Columbus and closed its station at the corner of Decatur and Water Streets, except for a single freight agent who continued operating it until the once-mighty Pennsy system went into total bankruptcy. The Pennsylvania was absorbed by ConRail which, in turn, abandoned all the remaining railroad tracks that ran along the waterfront.

So the Sandusky streetcars no longer picked up any passengers along Water Street. Such establishments as remained on the decaying waterfront were of such a character that patrons rarely took a streetcar to reach them.

The Lake Shore Electric system now faced another crisis. Not only did local streetcars use the Tiffin Avenue, Washington Street and Water Street tracks, but the interurbans bound to and from Toledo also used this route. The Lake Shore made a bold decision. The proprietors were not yet prepared to give up the once very lucrative Cleveland-Toledo traffic they had enjoyed. They decided to connect their track along Venice Road with the Columbus Avenue tracks.

The project was called the Perkins Avenue cut-off. New track was laid from Venice Road to the south side of Perkins Avenue at its intersection with Old Railroad. It is ironic that the name "Old Railroad" for that narrow county road which goes south several miles from Perkins Avenue came from the fact that it follows the line that once carried the original Mad River and Lake Erie track, Sandusky's first railroad. This track was abandoned sometime after the Civil War and new track was laid which was incorporated into the Big Four which, in turn, has now been abandoned and torn up.

In 1932, however, came a new railroad track to the corner of Old Railroad and Perkins Avenue, one destined to carry the Lake Shore interurbans along the south side of Perkins Avenue to the intersection of Columbus Avenue where a double switch was put in for the cars to turn north toward the city or south to the car barns.

All the young boys in town rode bicycles out to Perkins Avenue to watch the crews laying track for the interurbans. The laying of railroad track was something pictured in history books, particularly the joining of the tracks near Salt Lake City, Utah, in 1869 with a golden spike to mark completion of the first transcontinental rail line. By 1932, laying of track had almost become a lost art.

The event attracted national attention. Here was an electric railway laying new track instead of abandoning it. At the same time, Sandusky laid a new street which paralleled the cut-off from Perkins Avenue and Old Railroad to the Venice Road intersection, making it possible to drive directly out Perkins Avenue from Venice Road. This cut down mileage for quite a few automobile drivers as well. When the new streetcar track was put in service, public officials went out and cut a ribbon.

From then on, interurban cars instead of wending their way down Tiffin Avenue and on down to Water Street, ran along Perkins Avenue to Columbus and went down Columbus Avenue and back out. This cut several minutes from the time it took to get from Toledo to Cleveland. In addition to progress, however, it brought new danger. Motorists on Perkins Avenue sometimes forgot that the new interurban line had been put in place. The cars operated at a considerable rate of speed. In 1934, three members of the Popke family -- grandmother, daughter and granddaughter -- were instantly killed when they turned their car in front of an oncoming interurban car that they did not see. There were other fatal accidents.

In fact, interurban lines were rapidly going out of business because of expensive law suits in addition to declining patronage and rising maintenance costs. Railroads almost always went across the open country and had a grade crossing only every mile or two. Interurban lines often operated alongside highways and had two or three crossings per mile, plus perhaps half a dozen private driveways or more per mile. They also would swing out into the center of the street after operating alongside the road, and interurban cars moving in and out of the center of the street often sideswiped unattentive motorists.

The only liability insurance electric railways could obtain was so-called catastrophe insurance with the first $250,000 deductible, after which the insurer would pay between 60 and 80 percent of additional costs. Such insurance could keep a single wreck, such as derailment of a speeding interurban car with many injuries, from bankrupting the line.

However, even such liability insurance was becoming too expensive for the surviving electric railway lines to afford.

Automobiles were also adding to track maintenance costs. The more traffic there was on city streets, the more wear and tear there was on the tracks and especially on the switches. It also created an increasing problem in snowy winter weather.

The Lake Shore had big snowplow cars to keep its tracks free of snow and ice. These huge, tall, ungainly cars were built in the 1890s when the tracks were first laid and remained in service until the end. They had big brushes and blowers to sweep the snow up from the tracks and blow it aside. The snowplow cars made a lot of noise and, if you lived near a car line, as did this author in his Fulton Street home, you might be awakened at 4 a.m. on a dark winter morning by the noise of the snow plow. Immediately, you knew that the worst had happened -- a heavy snow had begun falling about midnight and things were going to be bad in the morning. Residents did not need to raise the window shade and look out. If the Lake Shore was operating its snow

A city streetcar helps to push a snowplow car as it struggles to keep the Depot loop line open on Camp Street on February 14, 1909. The crew, ready to shovel out deep places, stands by.

Hayes Presidential Center
Charles E. Frohman Collection

79

A Lake Shore Electric snowplow clears a heavy snowfall from the tracks on Columbus Avenue about 1905. The man on the car's roof stands ready to reattach the trolley every time it jumps the ice-covered wire. The noisy plows often had to work day and night to keep the tracks clear.

Hayes Presidential Center
Charles E. Frohman Collection

plows, it must be snowing hard and the plows were out to try to have the tracks clear so that those who needed to ride the streetcars to work or to school would find them running when daylight came.

At the same time, the plows would go out on the interurban lines and try to keep them clear of drifts.

Automobiles would grind snow and ice into the tracks, making it harder to keep them clear. In those days before snow tires, motorists often used chains, and the chains would get caught in the streetcar switches. A link that broke off could jam the switch or, even worse, derail an approaching streetcar.

In short, it became harder and harder to maintain the tracks and keep the cars running on time. It also became more expensive and this was really the last nail in the coffin of the interurban and streetcar era.

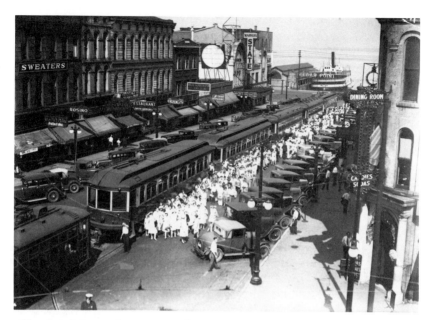

Chartered interurbans were always an exciting way to travel. Here on September 2, 1931, 400 members of 4-H Clubs from Huron County gather on Columbus Avenue in Sandusky to board five cars that were taking them back to Norwalk after an excursion to Cedar Point. In the background is the steamer G.A. Boeckling that had just brought them from the Point resort.

It was a great era that was coming to an end. There was always something a lot more fascinating about streetcars and interurbans than the motor buses which replaced them.

For example, when the First Congregational Church held its annual Sunday School picnic at Ruggles Beach, it was very exciting to see the big orange interurban car that had been chartered for the occasion coming up Columbus Avenue toward Jefferson Street. It bore a sign saying "Special" and had a white flag flying to mark it as a special chartered car.

With a shout of glee, all the children would rush to climb aboard and their mothers and fathers would follow, carrying the big picnic baskets loaded with food and baseball bats, croquet sets and other recreation equipment. Equally exciting was it at the end of the day to stand at the Ruggles Beach stop and wait for the interurban car with a white flag coming from the direction of Vermilion.

Somehow it just beats all hollow a bus pulling up to the curb. What is exciting about that?

Chartered interurban cars used to take Sandusky football fans to out-of-town games at Elyria, Lorain, Norwalk and Fremont, too.

Back in 1935 there was a really big game. Sandusky High School under coach Bob Whittaker, later coach at Bowling Green State University, had won 28 straight games. Teams like Norwalk and Bellevue were dropping off the Sandusky schedule and, for the first time, the Blue Streaks were going "big time" by playing a Toledo high school. The game was at Toledo Waite's field and the skeptics, of course, said this would be the end of Sandusky's winning streak, the longest in Ohio at that time.

Loyal fans disagreed and said Sandusky was going to show it really was the best team in the state. Three chartered interurban cars, jammed to the doors with fans, took off from Columbus Avenue a little more than two hours before the game. With Blue Streak banners flying, they left for the big game.

Sandusky won the game by a score that convinced every sports fan in Ohio. In fact, they overdid it, chasing the dazed Waite High School team virtually out of their own stadium by the score of 46 to 0.

When those fans arrived home at midnight, everyone in town knew it. Such singing and shouting as came from those three packed interurbans has rarely been equalled. They had made so much noise going through Fremont that the police in that unappreciative town had been called out to escort them as quickly as possible out of that city. The Fremont Ross fans had some inkling of what was going to happen to their team later on in the Sandusky schedule and it did, for the Blue Streaks went undefeated.

Those three chartered interurban cars somehow had more class than would three chartered buses.

We guess you might say that the interurbans had charisma. They were a glamorous and impressive means of transportation. But, alas, the automobile and the buses puffing their black, foul-smelling diesel exhausts were winning the race.

Chapter Nine

May 14, 1938: A Tearful Goodbye as the Last Cars Run

After discontinuance of the Tiffin Avenue streetcar line, another large abandonment soon took place in the Sandusky streetcar system.

In 1934, the East Monroe Street line was replaced by the city's first bus service. At the same time, what was left of the West Monroe Street line was also abandoned and service was discontinued on the entire eastern side of the Soldiers Home loop line.

In short, streetcars would no longer run on the East Market Street track from Wayne to Franklin Streets or on Franklin, East Madison and Hancock Streets, and the track along Milan Road from Scott Streets south all the way to the Soldiers Home would be abandoned as well as the East Monroe Street and First Street tracks.

On West Monroe Street, one car had shuttled back and forth between Superior and Camp Street, but this was no longer satisfactory for workers at the West End industrial plants, who were its principal patrons, and the bus service running from the East End all the way to the West End would prove more convenient.

Sandusky was left with just two streetcar lines. Two cars shuttling back and forth would maintain service between the Soldiers Home and downtown, operating on Columbus Avenue. At the Soldiers Home, the car, a double-ender, would simply reverse direction and return. Downtown, it could simply go around the block by way of Market, Wayne and Water Streets and head back up Columbus Avenue.

Meanwhile, the truncated Depot line still operated out Columbus Avenue to Hayes Avenue, across North Depot Street and down Camp to Washington Street where it reversed its trolley and returned. Two cars going back and forth operated that line.

Interurban service continued to both Cleveland and Toledo, with Limiteds every two hours and Locals restricted to two in the morning and two in the late afternoon.

The first morning Local was the "milk train" in the most literal sense of the term. At several points there were wooden platforms and before 7 a.m. farmers would bring their 10-gallon cans of milk, fresh from their dairy herds, and the cans would be rolled, top end up, aboard the baggage compartment which formed the front half of the Local car. The milk was brought to Sandusky where there were half a dozen dairies whose trucks would pick up the cans.

A number of men and women who lived on farms but held jobs in the city would use the Local to commute to work.The second Local picked up even more commuters and the rural students headed for Sandusky High School or the parochial schools and St. Mary's High School. The afternoon locals would take the workers and students home and also pick up more fresh produce, including boxes filled with iced fish fresh from Lay Brothers, Booth, Schact and other local commercial fishing fleets that then supplied delicious Lake Erie perch, caught that very day, to the Cleveland markets.

In the days before refrigeration, this fast service in bringing milk and perishable produce like eggs and fish to the cities was very important. Interurbans played a vital part in it before refrigerated trucks took their place and the small family farms that thrived in the Sandusky area were consolidated into large agricultural operations. Trucks were rapidly replacing the interurban service in delivery of all farm produce and light freight.

Many persons have forgotten that the interurbans, in addition to carrying passengers, for three or four decades also carried a significant amount of freight. The operation was called the Electric Package Service and became so successful that the Lake Shore ran several freight trains a day. While these ran mostly late at night after the passenger service ended, there often was at least one daytime train, as well.

The boxcars were painted a bright orange like the interurban cars. Usually, three or four, but never more than five, were coupled together behind a freight locomotive, itself a big orange car with two powerful electric motors.

Several sidings had been built along the Lake Shore's route where freight trains and locals could pull off to let the Limiteds pass so that the slow-moving freights did not delay the fast passenger service.

A large terminal was established in Sandusky for the Electric Package Service in an old stone building (later razed for a parking lot) on the east side of Wayne Street just north of Market Street. A spur track went back more than half the distance to Hancock Street.

It was fun to watch the freight trains switch the cars there. Whether the train had come in from Cleveland or Toledo, it would loop the block between Columbus Avenue and Wayne Street so as to be heading north on Wayne. If a car loaded with Sandusky freight was ready to be picked up, the freight train would go down to Water Street, back up on the spur track, hook onto the car and then back it up Wayne Street toward Market and leave it standing. Then the train would go forward and once again back up on the spur to leave a couple of cars of freight for Sandusky. Out onto Wayne Street it came once again and back up to couple on the car it had left standing. Then off to Cleveland the freight train would go. The switching of cars was done with great speed and efficiency so as not to interfere seriously with auto traffic.

The Electric Package Service was so fast that it was very competitive, for example, in bringing auto parts from Detroit, which for a while was a very big business. The only complaint Sanduskians had was that the freight trains rumbled rather loudly at night as they went down Columbus Avenue or out Tiffin Avenue. After the interurbans were gone, however, and freight went through Sandusky all night long whining in low gear, these people might have preferred the good old Lake Shore trains.

All the big interstate trucks in those days had to come through Sandusky by going all the way down to Washington Street and back out Huron Avenue in one direction or Tiffin Avenue in the other. They emitted heavy diesel fumes and tore up the streets. The construction of the Ohio Turnpike and the Route 2 bypass eventually let Sanduskians get a better night's sleep.

The Electric Package Service began to fade from competition from trucks because it could not make door-to-door

An Electric Package Service car which operated on the Lake Shore Electric line in the 1920's and 1930's. The car could carry as many as three or four boxcars behind it.

delivery. The whole Lake Shore system was struggling now. Although Sanduskians loved their little streetcars, they weren't riding them much any more.

The author remembers once about 1935 when he and a teenage friend decided to see if on our bicycles we could outrun a streetcar. We encountered a Depot line car reversing its trolley at Camp and Washington Streets for its return trip downtown, via Camp, North Depot, and Hayes and Columbus Avenues. We took off after him.

Bicycles had heavy balloon tires in those days and gearshifts were unknown, so bikes were by no means as fast as they are now. The streetcar made about 22 miles an hour with its throttle open and we could do no better than 12 to 15 miles an hour, puff as hard as we might. But, of course, the car had to stop from time to time to pick up passengers.

We soon found that patronage on the Depot line was discouragingly light. Even at the train depot, he picked up only two passengers. Had it not been for a couple of red stoplights, we might have had to give up the race. By the time he was on Hayes Avenue and we caught up at the Osborne Street light, the motorman knew what we were doing and he really opened his throttle, but a moving van backing into a driveway frustrated him and we caught up and took a slight lead. On Columbus Avenue, he overtook us and then beat us downtown by a full block.

During the course of the whole trip, he had picked up just eight passengers. At 12½ cents per token, that was one dollar in the fare box. Obviously, it cost more than that to operate the streetcar. We boys knew that there would not be streetcars much longer to race on Sandusky streets.

Sure enough, a few months later, the city of Sandusky decided that Hayes Avenue must be repaved. The question arose as to what to do about the streetcar tracks. The Lake Shore announced that it would discontinue the car line and replace it with bus service. This left Sandusky with only one remaining streetcar line, the Soldiers Home line, operated by two cars going back and forth on Columbus Avenue.

Soon the Lake Shore Electric Railway, like so many others throughout the nation, had to file for bankruptcy. On Saturday night, May 14, 1938, the end came. The last interurban car left Public Square in Cleveland, filled with nostalgic riders who tearfully sang "Auld Lang Syne" as they moved through Sandusky for the last time. A similar car left Toledo with passengers singing old songs as they rolled along and toasted with champagne. A fully loaded city streetcar carrying veterans singing "It's a Long Way to Tipperary" left the Soldiers Home and returned. The next day a bus took its place.

There was one more dying gasp from the Lake Shore. On Memorial Day, Monday May 30, since the wires were still up over the tracks, the Lake Shore ran two interurbans and three city streetcars to accommodate the Memorial Day parade and citizens who wished to visit graves of loved ones in Oakland Cemetery. Those were the final cars to run on San-dusky streets and to the Soldiers Home.

On the same day streetcar service stopped in Sandusky, it was an equally sad day in Norwalk. The interurban line that had operated between Fremont and Ceylon Junction was also discontinued. For Norwalk, it meant the loss of their little

Dinky, as they lovingly called the one streetcar that had shuttled back and forth for years on Main Street from one side of the city to the other.

For 33 years, Fred Grossman had been the operator of this car and he was one of Norwalk's best known and most beloved citizens. He was always willing to do favors for his customers.

The Cleveland Plain Dealer in a front page story on Sunday, May 15, told of Norwalk's loss and the extraordinary favors Grossman had done.

"It was nothing," said the Plain Dealer, "for a grandmother who was baby-sitting to wrap the baby up in warm blankets and hand it to Mr. Grossman, dropping a dime in the fare box, and have him hand it back to the mother, attending a card party ten blocks away, so she could nurse it and she would have it ready for him to carry back to the arms of the waiting grandmother on the next trip the Dinky took."

When some mischievous young boys painted the words "Toonerville Trolley" on the car one Halloween, so great was the indignation, said the Plain Dealer, that the culprits were apprehended and were made to apologize to Mr. Grossman and help wash the paint off. Norwalk was not going to permit its streetcar to be compared with the zany vehicle of the daily comic strips of that day called the "Toonerville Trolley," a word that has stuck in the language for an outdated piece of transportation equipment that was forever going off the tracks.

The streetcar and interurban era was over. All the cars were gathered into the car barns at Sandusky. The Lake Shore Coach Company began operating buses between Cleveland and Toledo, via Sandusky, that ran, at first, on about the same two-hour frequency of the electric Limiteds. Gradually patronage diminished for the buses too. In 1943, the Lake Shore Coach Company became part of the Ohio Rapid Transit lines of Newark, Ohio, which operated local bus service in Newark, Mansfield and other cities, and in 1949 the whole operation became a division of Greyhound Bus System. Eventually, all public transportation to Sandusky vanished, except for a daily Amtrak train on what is now called the ConRail system and operates the old New York Central tracks east and west from the city. Except for the coal-carrying Norfolk Southern (formerly Pennsylvania) line, all railroad tracks going south or southwest from Sandusky have been torn up.

From about 1915 to 1955 the Toonerville Trolley was the subject of a popular daily cartoon in many newspapers. The trolley line served a rural and growing suburban area around the town of "Toonerville." The jolly little motorman knew all his passengers personally and their foibles and follies were the butt of its humor. Artist Fontaine Fox created characters like Powerful Katrinka and joker Lem Wortle who became part of American folklore. The little car, forever late or jumping the track, symbolized the problems of early-day commuters. Today's commuters, caught in massive traffic jams, do not find their situation as funny or take it as philosophically as did the riders of the Toonerville Trolley.

The streetcar track laid almost a century ago is nowhere more evident than where it made a left turn onto East Water Street from Wayne Street. A thinning cover of asphalt on many Sandusky streets is bringing the old rails back to light.

Photograph 1988 by Glenn D. Everett

Today the role that streetcar transportation once played has been replaced by the institution known as the "car pool" in which workers who have cars pick up fellow employees who do not and share the commuting cost. Motorbikes and bicycles also play a significant role for younger workers who have not earned enough to purchase a car of their own. In the 1920s there were not more than a dozen adult men in Sandusky who rode bicyles to work. A bicycle was considered a child's toy. There were few motorcycles on the city streets and the light motorbike was unknown. So, in one way or another, the streetcar has been replaced.

When the Lake Shore Electric went out of business, the question arose as to what to do with its tracks. For the most part, the easiest answer was to cover them over with a layer of asphalt. That is why a majority of the tracks are still under Sandusky streets to this day. Telltale ripples

The rugged stone abutment that supported a short bridge across Sawmill Creek just south of the Lake Road may remain in place for many years to come. The interurban track ran on the right-of-way still visible behind the billboard. From here it ran four miles across fields straight to the center of the city of Huron.

Photograph 1988 by Glenn D. Everett

and cracks in the pavement often remind us of this. Eventually, problems will arise. The tracks were laid on wooden ties in the 1890s and these ties were cemented or bricked in place. They were heavily coated with creosote and decay very slowly, but being wood, they will eventually rot over a period of decades. Eventually, as some cities have already discovered,the surface of the street becomes rough as old washboard as the old wooden ties rot out underneath. This necessitates an expensive road repair job involving going down to dig out the old ties and rails and putting in a new concrete foundation for the center of the street.

However, it is encouraging to note how many of the old interurban poles remain. The trolley wires, of course, were quickly removed, the copper wire having salvage value. The poles were left in place. The Lake Shore had derived considerable revenue by letting electric utilities and telephone companies along its routes string their wires on its interurban poles.

Along the west side of Milan Road, for example, the interurban poles can be distinguished by their unusual height. They were so tall because the big double-deck interurban cars had to pass beneath them and the trolley wire was attached to the pole by brackets that extended high over the track. Then the electric utility wires were added up above that. These poles which have been in the ground now for nearly 100 years still appear very durable.

The salvagers quickly pulled up the steel rails out in the open country, either selling them to railroads as replacements for broken rails or sending them to the steel mills for scrap. The small bridges that carried the interurban tracks over streams and brooks were at first left in place, but yielded to scrap hunters during the patriotic steel salvage drives of World War II (1941-45). However, the stone abutments that supported these bridges were left largely untouched. So strong was the work of the stonemasons of the 1890s that these abutments may remain in place for centuries like the ruins of old Roman aqueducts in Europe unless someone wants to go to some considerable trouble tearing them out.

The wooden ties out in the country were, at first, left undisturbed. This was for a good reason. They were very hard to dig out. The author's uncle, G.W. Wolff, who was building a house opposite the Plum Brook Country Club on Hull Road just as the interurbans passed into history, made a sharp deal with the Lake Shore's receiver in bankruptcy. He was told he could dig up 100 ties for only a nickle apiece to make fencing for his gardens and build a patio. The ties were excellent for this purpose but after he had spent a week digging out only a dozen with pick and shovel, the project was abandoned.

After World War II came a new invention, the now common backhoe. With one of those hoes, ties could be dug up with a few minutes effort. Nursery owners had found that customers would pay as much as $5 apiece for the heavy 50-pound creosoted ties which were, indeed, very useful in building gardens and terraces. Soon nearly all the interurban ties found new homes.

A sad sight — an abandoned railroad track, once the main line of the Lake Erie and Western, where it crossed Sandusky County Road 32 in the once-bustling village of Erlin. The Lake Shore interurban approached 100 yards to the south, its poles still visible at far right. From this point the interurban ran parallel to the railroad for 12 miles through Castalia to Sandusky. The last train ran on this track over 30 years ago.

Photograph 1988 by Glenn D. Everett

Nowadays when railroads are abandoned -- and hundreds of miles of track have been in Ohio -- large bulldozers come along and lift off the rails and tear out the ties. The track owners have found out that the old ties can be a valuable commodity.

Still left behind, however, are often the big steel spikes that held the rails to the ties. Recently, a Boy Scout troop, armed with a metal detector, went along an old railroad right-of-way and dug up over 1,000 pounds of such spikes, enough to buy a new set of camping equipment for the troop.

What about the big interurban cars? Most of them found new homes, too. They were destined to inaugurate a whole new concept in American life -- the fast-food diner. The heavy metal wheels were removed and cut up for scrap but the body, with inside seats ripped out and replaced by a long counter and stools, could become a roadside diner. The cook worked up in the old baggage compartment. Waitresses served the customers along the lengthy counter. The little restrooms in the rear of the cars (which had borne big signs "Please Do Not Flush While on City Streets or Standing in Station") were hooked up to plumbing and continued in use.

In fact, these roadside diners became so popular in the 1930s and '40s that imitation diners were soon manufactured, the supply of retired interurban cars having been quickly exhausted. They were made to look like old streetcars, but were wider, so as to give both customers and waitresses more room, and had large cooking facilities. The diner soon became an American institution.

Oh, but so successful were the old interurban cars in their new role in America that they soon attracted competition. Along came McDonald's, Burger King and a host of other fast food outlets, much larger and faster in service than any of the old diners. And so the old interurbans which had yielded to competition of the automobiles had to yield again. We could not find a single old diner -- real or imitation -- left in business to photograph for this book.

A few of the cars survived intact in the hands of collectors, and old streetcar museums with operating antique cars have become a popular tourist attraction in several areas of the nation. Like antique automobiles, they are worth thousands of dollars today.

The little streetcars that ran on Sandusky streets were made of metal, and all were scrapped in the World War II steel salvage drive. The old wooden cars were simply burned, alas, and their metal fittings salvaged from the ashes.

The freight cars of the Electric Package Service found new homes as barns and storage sheds for those willing to buy them for a few dollars and haul them away. A few may still survive, although they are probably hard to distinguish in appearance from other sheds today.

All that remains of the Lake Shore Electric Railroad are the vestiges of its tracks peeking up from city streets and the places on the old right-of-way out in the countryside where cuts were made through hillsides or embankments were made to carry the tracks across low valleys. These and the stone bridge abutments remain indelible. If you know where to look, it is fun to practice a little modern archeology by finding the remains of this once-great transportation system.

The big orange cars no longer flash by. The clanging bell of the city streetcars has been stilled. They were part of a great and romantic era of our advancing civilization. Like the puffing steam engines of the old-time railroads, they are gone but will never be forgotten. They will always be a source of fascination to generations that have not been able to experience the adventure of riding them.